THIS BOOK ~~~~ TAKE YOUR
PRAYER ~~~~ ~~VELS!~~
DO IT UP!

WE LOVE YOU!
THE YOUTH TEAM
MPUMC

THE BOOK OF EVERYDAY PRAYER
Liturgies for Daily Devotion

By Jeremy Steele

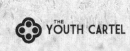

THE
YOUTH CARTEL

THE BOOK OF EVERYDAY PRAYER

Copyright © 2017 by Jeremy Steele

Publisher: Mark Oestreicher
Managing Editor: Tamara Rice
Cover Design: Adam McLane
Layout: Marilee R. Pankratz
Creative Director: Numa Tology

ISBN-13: 978-1-942145-34-9
ISBN-10: 1-942145-34-9

The Youth Cartel, LLC
www.theyouthcartel.com
Email: info@theyouthcartel.com
Born in San Diego
Printed in the U.S.A

To Mom.
Now I lay me down to sleep...

CONTENTS

WHY A PRAYER BOOK?
(HOW TO USE THIS THING)

Have you ever felt like you wanted to pray about something that just happened but weren't sure what to say? Or, have you had a moment in the middle of the day or night where you thought that you'd like to spend some time with God but weren't sure what to do? This book is for those moments.

That feeling of wanting to pray or to spend time with God is the Holy Spirit, and it is one of the great gifts of our relationship with him. However, it can be a little intimidating to just start praying the first thing that comes into your head. When you add in the fact that you are trying to express your heart to the God of the universe, even your best spontaneous prayers might sometimes seem like they don't really capture what you are feeling.

When that happens, prayers can take a weird turn into a sort of genie-in-the-bottle thing or a request line for magical cures. We might go on and on, asking God to do this and heal that, missing out on the real power of prayer. Prayer is a conversation with God. It's more than a chance to convince the Ultimate Power to grant your wish for a million dollars. (Though we all know the first wish needs to be for more wishes.)

That's why for centuries Christians have used prayer books. They give us a place to start our time with God and offer us words to help express our hearts to God. This book has a few different sections that can help you:

Praying Throughout the Day: Praying the Hours
Right Words for the Right Time: Prayers for Every Occasion
Less Words, More Prayer: Ancient Prayer Practices
My Prayers: Blank Pages for Personal Prayers

I'm going to give you some tips for using each of these sections, but there's no one correct way. Use them however you want.

PRAYING THROUGHOUT THE DAY

The practice of praying at different times throughout the day is one of the most ancient tools we have in the spiritual life. In fact, the writer of Psalm 119 says, "Seven times a day I praise you for your righteous laws" (Psalm 119:164, NIV). Scholars believe this is an indication that the practice of praying throughout the day at specific times was already happening when the Psalms were being written.

I won't go into all the history, but just google "Fixed Hour Prayer" and you can read all you want. Now, let's get to how you can use it.

When you have time to spend with God, open the book.
The first question I was asked when I was telling a friend about this book was, "Wait, are you expecting people to, like, set some alarm on their phones and stop wherever they are, like in the middle of their conversations, and say these prayers? And then do it again at the next time and the next?" *No.* That would be kind of cool but mostly weird. Though that's not far from how Christian monks practice it, you aren't a monk, and I don't expect six prayer times every day to ever really happen for you... unless you do a special prayer retreat. (See **Using This Book in a Group Setting** on page 203.)

My hope is that you will keep this book with you. When you realize you have a couple minutes to spend with God, you can take it out and find a prayer experience that is designed to help you offer prayers that make sense based on the day of the week and the moment in the day. I've written the prayers for six different times of the day: Dawn, Morning, Noonday, Afternoon, Evening, Midnight.

In each time of prayer, you will see the following elements:

- **Call to Prayer:** There's a moment in the book of Luke where a crowd of people are singing praises to Jesus the way they would to God. When the religious leaders of that time hear this, they tell Jesus that he should make the crowd stop singing. Jesus replies that "If they kept quiet, the stones along the road would burst into cheers!" (Luke 19:40). There is something deep within us that calls us to prayer. The call to prayer reminds us that we pray not because we want something but because God is worthy of prayer and there is something within us that longs to reach out and connect. Generally, these calls to prayer reflect something about God that is worthy of praise.

- **Invitation:** From the earliest days, when people began praying to God, they asked God to be present. Sometimes in Scripture we see people asking God to remember his covenant and sometimes we see his people just crying out, asking God to listen. The Invitation asks for God to be present, to listen, and to respond.

- **Confession**: When we enter God's presence, we immediately come face to face with our own brokenness. That's why we confess. We tell God our sins and ask for forgiveness. Several of these prayer experiences have a time for you to take a moment to think through your sins and confess them specifically, while others offer a time of more general confession.

- **Refrain:** Like our heartbeats give the rhythm to our bodies (and even our music, but that's another book altogether), the refrain gives a rhythm to our prayer. It gives focus and grounds the rest of the prayer. As you read, think of how the refrain connects to the Reading and the Psalm and the rest of the elements.

- **Reading:** Prayer is a two-way street. We talk to God, but God also talks to us. When God speaks, it can come to us as a thought in our heads, but it can also be through the words of another person or in something we read (especially the Bible). Think of the reading as one of the ways that God could be speaking to you. Ask yourself: *How is this reading challenging me? What does it call me to do?*

- **Psalm:** Art helps us express things that are bigger than we are. It helps us express our love, our fears, and our biggest hopes. This section takes poetry composed by brilliant writers throughout history to help us reach out and express our hearts to God.

- **The Lord's Prayer:** Jesus taught his disciples a very specific, very short prayer (Matthew 6:9-13) that Christians have been using for the last two thousand years, and every prayer service incorporates it here. I have chosen to print it here in the older form of English (adapted from *The Book of Common Prayer*). I've done that because even though Jesus didn't teach the prayer in English, the older sounding words help remind us that we are saying a prayer that is very old; in fact, it is the oldest

Christian prayer we have.

- **Today's Prayer:** Each day has a prayer that's tied to that specific moment in the week and helps express a hope and challenge for that exact time.

- **Concluding Prayer:** Each service also concludes with a prayer that tries to express something specific for that time of the day on that day of the week. You'll find that Evening Prayers often talk about going to sleep while Dawn Prayers talk about the beginning of a new day.

So, how do you do these prayer experiences? Here are a couple of tips from people who have tried them out.

Don't be intimidated by the language.

Depending on your church, the language in these prayers might seem formal—not to mention the fact that you'll be praying prayers that someone else has written! I get that, but try them anyway. Much like green eggs and ham, you might find that using this language isn't so bad and can help you express things that have always been difficult to put words to. You might even find that you have spent most of your prayer time treating God more like a magic wish-granting Santa than a friend or mentor who is fun to spend time with.

You'll also find some very old words here written by people who lived a long time ago. I've done my best to make them understandable. They are here because we have an old faith. And when we pray, we are part of a long stream of faith that stretches for millennia. Using these old prayers and poems connects us to our history as we say words that people have been using for hundreds of years to express their hearts to God.

Try speaking the prayers out loud.

After I gave the first set of these to a group I lead in the upstairs of a local coffee shop each week, they came back and all had the same advice: *Say the prayers out loud.* For most of the people, saying the prayers out loud helped them make the prayers their own because they could speak them with emotion. When they said the prayers to themselves, it felt as if they were just reading prayers written by someone else.

Speaking them out loud also can help you keep your focus. For some reason, it's easier to get distracted from the prayer service when it's all in your head than when you are speaking it out loud.

Don't treat prayer like a task, it's a conversation.

If you aren't careful, you'll find yourself treating these like tasks you need to complete rather than conversations. One of the most important things to keep in mind about prayer is that it's a dialogue. We speak, and we listen. That means that you need to go slow and take significant pauses throughout each of these prayer experiences to listen to God and center yourself. Don't rush. Don't blow through the movements of prayer. Take your time. It's better to not finish than to reach the end without ever stopping to listen.

Where should you pause? You can pause wherever you want, but each service is divided up into different sections, movements, or elements as outlined earlier in the introduction (Call to Prayer, Invitation, Refrain, etc.). Before you move from one section to another, take a break and listen for as long as you can. One person told me she liked to listen for twice as long as it took her to say the prayer. Another person told me she set a timer for one minute over and over again. Pause for as long as you want, but make sure you stop to listen in between each of these moments.

Challenge yourself to increase the number of prayer times per day.

We all have a tendency to keep God in a "church box," only paying attention to our faith when we are at church. That's one of the reasons people have been practicing fixed-hour prayers like these for millennia. When you take a moment to pray several times throughout your day, you get in the habit of being aware of God's presence everywhere and at all times.

Though it would be *very* difficult to do all of these prayer experiences every day, it's probably very easy for you to do one or two per day—and, if you try, to add a third. That's part of why I included so many of the traditional hours: I wanted you to feel like you had a prayer experience that was just right basically any time of the day or night. Making it your goal to increase the number of these you do each day in any given week might be one of the most spiritually significant things you ever choose to do.

Add your own words and/or some of the Right Words for the Right Time prayers as you go along.

Don't feel like you have to say exactly what's printed on the page. Add your own prayers to the ones in black and white so that you can express what's weighing on your heart to God. And, if you're not sure where to start, take a look at the prayers in **Right Words for the Right Time** (page 177) and add one of those.

Adding those prayers can take these experiences to the next level for you. For example, you might pull out the book right after your boyfriend or girlfriend has broken up with you, when you know you need to spend time with God but don't really feel like reading a more formal prayer. Just flip to the "After the Breakup" prayer (page 184) and say the words that seem to fit.

RIGHT WORDS FOR THE RIGHT TIME

I remember the first time someone gave me a prayer book that had prayers for specific moments. I remember it because I was really struggling with a friend who was moving away and felt like I wanted to pray to God but didn't know where to start. When I scanned the table of contents, I saw that exact subject. I immediately flipped to the prayer. I felt like I could begin praying about it for the first time since I found out about my friend moving.

Look through the prayers now.

These prayers can be a lot of fun to read, even if you don't particularly need them right now. And reading them now can help you remember that they exist when the moment happens. So, take a second right now and read a couple. I'll wait here until you get back. (But do come back, because I have a couple of tips about these prayers too.)

Use these prayers as a starting place.

These prayers are fine in and of themselves, but if you let them, they can be like turning the key in your own prayer engine. They are a great place to start. Feel free to use them as the beginning of your time of prayer and then add your own words, change mine, or both.

LESS WORDS, MORE PRAYER

Sometimes words get in the way of connecting with God. Ultimately prayer is a spiritual thing, and many Christians throughout the ages have felt that they needed less words to be able to connect with God. To be more accurate, they felt that the words we use are more like a scaffolding on which we climb to connect with him. These Christian mystics spent their lives discovering and practicing a life of prayer that used words in a different way as they reached out to connect with their Creator. This chapter gives you a handful of the practices they discovered that have lasted throughout the centuries. They include:

Centering Prayer
The Jesus Prayer
Lectio Divina
Ignatian Examen

WRITE YOUR OWN PRAYERS

Writing prayers for specific moments can be both helpful and fun. If you are in a creative writing mood, take a moment and think of a moment or situation that I haven't already written about and write your own prayer. We've even added space for that at the back of the book. (See 211.) Not only will this be fun for you, but when you are finished, you'll have that prayer when that specific moment comes up later in your life. (And, if you'd like to share that prayer with others, send me an email here: **moreeverydayprayer@gmail.com**. I'll post it on **jeremywords.com/prayers**.)

That's it. Those are all my tips. Think of this book as a sort of prayer Swiss Army knife. It has a bunch of tools for different jobs, and if you keep it around, you'll have just what you need when you're ready to get to work. It's my hope that this book will transform your prayer life. I pray that it will break you out of the rut of saying the same three sentences every night and help you learn how to have real conversations with God.

PRAYING
THROUGHOUT THE DAY

MONDAY

DAWN PRAYER

Call to Prayer:
The universe is filled with your presence. As the universe expands, galaxies spin and planets orbit their stars. All of your works declare your glory.

Invitation:
O LORD, hear me as I pray;
    pay attention to my groaning.
Listen to my cry for help, my King and my God,
    for I pray to no one but you.
Listen to my voice in the morning, LORD.
Each morning I bring my requests to you and wait expectantly.

Psalm 5:1-3

Refrain:
Open my eyes! Open my heart! Let my soul recognize your voice!

Reading:
At dawn Jesus was standing on the beach, but the disciples couldn't see who he was. He called out, "Fellows, have you caught any fish?"

"No," they replied.

Then he said, "Throw out your net on the right-hand side of the boat, and you'll get some!" So they did, and they couldn't haul in the net because there were so many fish in it.

Then the disciple Jesus loved said to Peter, "It's the Lord!" When Simon Peter heard that it was the Lord, he put on his tunic (for he had stripped for work), jumped into the water, and headed to shore. The others stayed with the boat and pulled the loaded net to the shore, for they were only about a hundred yards from shore. When they got there, they found breakfast waiting for them—fish cooking over a charcoal fire, and some bread.

"Bring some of the fish you've just caught," Jesus said. So Simon Peter went aboard and dragged the net to the shore. There were 153 large fish, and yet the net hadn't torn.

"Now come and have some breakfast!" Jesus said. None of the

disciples dared to ask him, "Who are you?" They knew it was the
Lord. Then Jesus served them the bread and the fish. This was the
third time Jesus had appeared to his disciples since he had been
raised from the dead.

After breakfast Jesus asked Simon Peter, "Simon son of John, do
you love me more than these?"

"Yes, Lord," Peter replied, "you know I love you."

"Then feed my lambs," Jesus told him.

Jesus repeated the question: "Simon son of John,
do you love me?"

"Yes, Lord," Peter said, "you know I love you."

"Then take care of my sheep," Jesus said.

A third time he asked him, "Simon son of John,
do you love me?"

Peter was hurt that Jesus asked the question a third time.
He said, "Lord, you know everything. You know that I love you."

Jesus said, "Then feed my sheep..."

John 21:4-17

Refrain:
Open my eyes! Open my heart! Let my soul recognize your voice!

Psalm:
The King shall come when morning dawns
and light triumphant breaks,
when beauty gilds the eastern hills
and life to joy awakes.

Not, as of old, a little child,
to bear and fight and die,
but crowned with glory like the sun
that lights the morning sky.

Brighter than the rising morning
when Christ, victorious, rose
and left the lonesome place of death,
despite the rage of foes.

Brighter than that glorious morning
shall dawn upon our race
the day when Christ in splendor comes
and we shall see his face.

The King shall come when morning dawns
and light and beauty brings.
Hail, Christ the Lord! Your people pray:
Come quickly, King of kings.

"The King Shall Come When Morning Dawns"
by John Brownlie, late 1800s
(author's adaptation)

Refrain:
Open my eyes! Open my heart! Let my soul recognize your voice!

The Lord's Prayer:
Our Father, who art in heaven,
Hallowed be thy name.
Thy kingdom come,
Thy will be done on earth,
As it is in heaven.
Give us this day our daily bread.
And forgive us our sins, as we forgive those who sin against us.
And lead us not into temptation, but deliver us from evil.
For thine is the kingdom, and the power, and the glory,
forever and ever.

Today's Prayer:
Your Word is clear that everything we have is a gift from you. Every
piece of technology, every bite of food we eat, every sip we take of our
favorite drink, and every minute we live: They are all gifts from you.
Help me on this Monday to see all these things as gifts. Help me not
miss them as I get back into the swing of things. Help me see my life
is filled with your gifts and is meant to be offered as a gift back to you
through how I live and use all the gifts you have given me. Help me to
make this day a gift to your world.

Concluding Prayer:
Holy Creator God, you have brought me safely to the beginning of this day. Give me grace to see you through the fog of tasks ahead of me. Put me to doing, put me to suffering. I offer this day completely to you and ask that you hide me in the hollow of your arms and pull me back when I venture too close to the quicksand of sin so that this day helps your kingdom come and your will be done on earth as it is in heaven. *Amen.*

MORNING PRAYER

Call to Prayer:
Open my eyes with the morning light. Let me see your face. Let me hear you speak.

Confession:
All gracious and most merciful God,
I have made mistakes; I continue to make them.
I have listened to my own guidance over yours;
I have turned away from your path;
I have seen the sparkle of sin and lost focus.
I have sinned.
I have sinned by my actions.
I have sinned by my inaction.

God, have mercy on me,
according to your promises in Jesus Christ.

In your mercy, give me grace
to follow your guidance, to stay on your path,
to ignore the allure of sin and live a holy life beyond what I can do myself.

Invitation:
Come, my children, and listen to me, and I will teach you to fear the LORD.

Psalm 34:11

Refrain:
Sing to the LORD, all you godly ones!
    Praise his holy name.
For his anger lasts only a moment,
    but his favor lasts a lifetime!
Weeping may last through the night,
    but joy comes with the morning.

Psalm 30:4-5

Reading:

One day some people said to Jesus, "John the Baptist's disciples fast
and pray regularly, and so do the disciples of the Pharisees. Why are
your disciples always eating and drinking?"

Jesus responded, "Do wedding guests fast while celebrating with
the groom? Of course not. But someday the groom will be taken away
from them, and then they will fast."

Then Jesus gave them this illustration: "No one tears a piece of
cloth from a new garment and uses it to patch an old garment. For
then the new garment would be ruined, and the new patch wouldn't
even match the old garment.

"And no one puts new wine into old wineskins. For the new
wine would burst the wineskins, spilling the wine and ruining the
skins. New wine must be stored in new wineskins. But no one who
drinks the old wine seems to want the new wine. 'The old is just fine,'
they say."

Luke 5:33-39

Refrain:

Sing to the LORD, all you godly ones!
    Praise his holy name.
For his anger lasts only a moment,
    but his favor lasts a lifetime!
Weeping may last through the night,
    but joy comes with the morning.

Psalm 30:4-5

Psalm

Christ, whose glory fills the skies,
Christ, the true, the only light.
Sun of Righteousness, arise;
Triumph over the shades of night.
Day-spring from on high, be near;
Day-star, in my heart appear.

Dark and cheerless is the morn
Unaccompanied by thee.
Joyless is the day's return,

Till your mercy's beams I see.
Till your inward light impart,
Glad my eyes and warm my heart.

Visit then this soul of mine,
Pierce the gloom of sin and grief.
Fill me, Radiancy Divine.
Scatter all my unbelief,
More and more yourself display,
Shining to the perfect day.

"Morning Hymn"
by Charles Wesley, 1740
(author's adaptation)

Refrain:
Sing to the LORD, all you godly ones!
　　Praise his holy name.
For his anger lasts only a moment,
　　but his favor lasts a lifetime!
Weeping may last through the night,
　　but joy comes with the morning.

Psalm 30:4-5

The Lord's Prayer:
Our Father, who art in heaven,
Hallowed be thy name.
Thy kingdom come,
Thy will be done on earth,
As it is in heaven.
Give us this day our daily bread.
And forgive us our sins, as we forgive those who sin against us.
And lead us not into temptation, but deliver us from evil.
For thine is the kingdom, and the power, and the glory,
forever and ever.

Today's Prayer:
Your Word is clear that everything we have is a gift from you. Every piece of technology, every bite of food we eat, every sip we take of our favorite drink, and every minute we live: They are all gifts from you. Help me on this Monday to see all these things as gifts. Help me not miss them as I get back into the swing of things. Help me see my life is filled with your gifts and is meant to be offered as a gift back to you through how I live and use all the gifts you have given me. Help me to make this day a gift to your world.

Concluding Prayer:
O Lord, our heavenly Father, almighty and everlasting God, who has brought me safely to the beginning of this day: Defend me with your mighty power; empower me to not fall into sin or run into any kind of danger but to do what is right in your eyes, through Jesus Christ my Lord. *Amen.*

NOONDAY PRAYER

Call to Prayer:
Send your word to me. Let its sound call my soul to listen.

Invitation:
The Lord has given us his word. Let us come to him.

Refrain:
The LORD is good and does what is right;
  He shows the proper path to those who go astray.

Psalm 25:8

Psalm:
Holy Spirit, come with power;
Let your light, in darkest hour,
Shine upon our traveling way.
Father of the humble heart,
Come, your choicest gifts impart—
Illumine our hearts with heavenly ray.

You can our hearts console;
Sweet the time spent with the soul—
Cooling breath at noon of day,
Calm your rest in toil and care
Soft your shade in noontime glare—
You do chase our tears away.

Veni, Sancte Spiritus Et Emitte Caelitus or "Golden Sequence"
Mass for Pentecost, Eleventh-Century
(author's adaptation)

Refrain:
The LORD is good and does what is right;
  He shows the proper path to those who go astray.

Psalm 25:8

The Lord's Prayer:

Our Father, who art in heaven,
Hallowed be thy name.
Thy kingdom come,
Thy will be done on earth,
As it is in heaven.
Give us this day our daily bread.
And forgive us our sins, as we forgive those who sin against us.
And lead us not into temptation, but deliver us from evil.
For thine is the kingdom, and the power, and the glory,
forever and ever.

Today's Prayer:

Your Word is clear that everything we have is a gift from you. Every piece of technology, every bite of food we eat, every sip we take of our favorite drink, and every minute we live: They are all gifts from you. Help me on this Monday to see all these things as gifts. Help me not miss them as I get back into the swing of things. Help me see my life is filled with your gifts and is meant to be offered as a gift back to you through how I live and use all the gifts you have given me. Help me to make this day a gift to your world.

Concluding Prayer:

All-knowing and everlasting God, who spoke honestly with the woman at the well at noon, as I come to the middle of this day I pray that you would be honest with me and let me find truth in your words as they are spoken to me through your people this day. I pray that you would be honest with me and let me hear your words wherever you speak them, because you have the words of life forever and ever. *Amen.*

AFTERNOON/AFTER SCHOOL PRAYER

Call to Prayer:
The LORD looks down from heaven
  on the entire human race;
he looks to see if anyone is truly wise,
  if anyone seeks God.

Psalm 14:2

Confession
Merciful God,
I find myself in the in the afternoon already in need of forgiveness.
I want to be faithful. I want to do what is right.
  But I have done what I did not want to do
  again.
Forgive me for these sins and those that I cannot remember.

Confess your specific sins to God.

In the name of Jesus Christ, I pray.

Invitation:
Praise the God who forgives,
  who forgives again,
  who forgives forever.

Refrain:
O LORD, hear my plea for justice.
  Listen to my cry for help.
Pay attention to my prayer,
  for it comes from honest lips.

Psalm 17:1

Reading:

Late in the afternoon his disciples came to him and said, "This is a remote place, and it's already getting late. Send the crowds away so they can go to the nearby farms and villages and buy something to eat."

But Jesus said, "You feed them."

"With what?" they asked. "We'd have to work for months to earn enough money to buy food for all these people!"

"How much bread do you have?" he asked. "Go and find out."

They came back and reported, "We have five loaves of bread and two fish."

Then Jesus told the disciples to have the people sit down in groups on the green grass. So they sat down in groups of fifty or a hundred.

Jesus took the five loaves and two fish, looked up toward heaven, and blessed them. Then, breaking the loaves into pieces, he kept giving the bread to the disciples so they could distribute it to the people. He also divided the fish for everyone to share. They all ate as much as they wanted, and afterward, the disciples picked up twelve baskets of leftover bread and fish. A total of 5,000 men and their families were fed.

Mark 6:35-44

Refrain:

O LORD, hear my plea for justice.
    Listen to my cry for help.
Pay attention to my prayer,
    for it comes from honest lips.

Psalm 17:1

Psalm:

Now sinks the glowing orb of day,
And silent night comes on with haste;
So gains our life the appointed goal,
That marks the limit of our race.

O Christ, uplifted on the Cross!
Thine arms were stretched towards the sky.
Grant us with love that Cross to seek,
And folded in those arms to die.

Now to the Father enthroned on high,
And to Christ his only Son,
And to the Spirit, glory be,
Now, and while endless ages run.

Labente Jam Solis Rotá
by Charles Coffin, 1700s
(author's adaptation)

Refrain:

O LORD, hear my plea for justice.
Listen to my cry for help.
Pay attention to my prayer,
for it comes from honest lips.

Psalm 17:1

The Lord's Prayer:

Our Father, who art in heaven,
Hallowed be thy name.
Thy kingdom come,
Thy will be done on earth,
As it is in heaven.
Give us this day our daily bread.
And forgive us our sins, as we forgive those who sin against us.
And lead us not into temptation, but deliver us from evil.
For thine is the kingdom, and the power, and the glory,
forever and ever.

Today's Prayer:
Your Word is clear that everything we have is a gift from you. Every piece of technology, every bite of food we eat, every sip we take of our favorite drink, and every minute we live: They are all gifts from you. Help me on this Monday to see all these things as gifts. Help me not miss them as I get back into the swing of things. Help me see my life is filled with your gifts and is meant to be offered as a gift back to you through how I live and use all the gifts you have given me. Help me to make this day a gift to your world.

Concluding Prayer:
God, you were with me when I awoke this morning, and as I continue on moving towards this day's end, let me not forget that you are with me. Guide my steps as I seek to follow your lead and protect me from those who may be working against me. Make me an agent of your grace in the hours that remain. *Amen.*

END OF DAY PRAYER

Call to Prayer:
The Lord Almighty grant me a peaceful night and a perfect end.
from The Book of Common Prayer

Confession:
Creator, Savior, Spirit, I have sinned.
You were there
    as I turned a blind eye to people in need.
You heard me
    speak words that brought pain instead of love.
You saw me
    shrink from defending the righteous.
Forgive me for all the moments I slipped off of the path;
Forgive me for all the gifts I didn't notice;
Forgive me, heal me,
    And raise me to new life again.

Invitation:
Hear me as I pray, O LORD.
    Be merciful and answer me!
Psalm 27:7

Refrain:
Send your angels to sing songs of peace over me as I sleep and guard me until I rise again with you.

Reading:
"I will make a covenant of peace with my people and drive away the dangerous animals from the land. Then they will be able to camp safely in the wildest places and sleep in the woods without fear. I will bless my people and their homes around my holy hill. And in the proper season I will send the showers they need. There will be showers of blessing. The orchards and fields of my people will yield bumper crops, and everyone will live in safety. When I have broken their chains of slavery and rescued them from those who enslaved

them, then they will know that I am the LORD. They will no longer be prey for other nations, and wild animals will no longer devour them. They will live in safety, and no one will frighten them.

"And I will make their land famous for its crops, so my people will never again suffer from famines or the insults of foreign nations. In this way, they will know that I, the LORD their God, am with them. And they will know that they, the people of Israel, are my people, says the Sovereign LORD. You are my flock, the sheep of my pasture. You are my people, and I am your God. I, the Sovereign LORD, have spoken!"

Ezekiel 34:25-31

Refrain:

In peace I will lie down and sleep,
    for you alone, LORD,
      make me dwell in safety.

Psalm 4:8 (NIV)

Psalm:

Sleep that soothingly restores
Weary nature's wasted powers,
Gift of an indulgent God
Bestow it on your child this night.

Jesus, Lord, we cry to thee
Friend of helpless infancy,
Now the sufferer's grief suspend,
Now the balmy blessing send.

In the arms of faith and prayer
Whom to you we humbly bear,
Safe in your protection keep,
Let him on your shoulder sleep.

Touched yourself with human pain,
Sympathizing Son of Man,
Ease the anguish of his chest,
Lull him in your arms to rest.

Object of your dearest love
Hide his precious life above,
Precious in the sight of God,
Dearly bought with all thy blood.

Him, we to your grace commend,
Confident you will defend,
Till the answered prayer is sealed,
Till the child of faith is healed.

"For Sleep"
by Charles Wesley, 1700s
(author's adaptation)

Refrain:
In peace I will lie down and sleep,
    for you alone, LORD,
    make me dwell in safety.

Psalm 4:8 (NIV)

The Lord's Prayer:
Our Father, who art in heaven,
Hallowed be thy name.
Thy kingdom come,
Thy will be done on earth,
As it is in heaven.
Give us this day our daily bread.
And forgive us our sins, as we forgive those who sin against us.
And lead us not into temptation, but deliver us from evil.
For thine is the kingdom, and the power, and the glory,
forever and ever.

Today's Prayer:
Your Word is clear that everything we have is a gift from you. Every
piece of technology, every bite of food we eat, every sip we take of our
favorite drink, and every minute we live: They are all gifts from you.
Help me on this Monday to see all these things as gifts. Help me not
miss them as I get back into the swing of things. Help me see my life
is filled with your gifts and is meant to be offered as a gift back to you

through how I live and use all the gifts you have given me. Help me to make this day a gift to your world.

Concluding Prayer:

Though my world maybe dark, dispel its evil with your light. Fill my dreams with the presence of your love and protect me from all the concerns of this night through the power of your name. *Amen.*

MIDNIGHT PRAYER

Call to Prayer:
Arise from your slumber; awake to the presence of God!
Blessed is the one who stays with the Lord
    Even when night comes,
    Even when darkness reigns.
In the deepest night, we do not fear,
    Because God is with us,
    And we are with God
Even in the night.

Invitation:
I pray to you, O LORD, my rock.
    Do not turn a deaf ear to me.
For if you are silent,
    I might as well give up and die.
Listen to my prayer for mercy
    as I cry out to you for help,
    as I lift my hands toward your holy sanctuary.

                                            Psalm 28:1-2

Refrain:
Lord, let me see in the darkness.
    Show me the light of life.

Reading:
Therefore, since God in his mercy has given us this new way, we never give up. We reject all shameful deeds and underhanded methods. We don't try to trick anyone or distort the word of God. We tell the truth before God, and all who are honest know this.

If the Good News we preach is hidden behind a veil, it is hidden only from people who are perishing. Satan, who is the god of this world, has blinded the minds of those who don't believe. They are unable to see the glorious light of the Good News. They don't understand this message about the glory of Christ, who is the exact likeness of God.

You see, we don't go around preaching about ourselves. We preach that Jesus Christ is Lord, and we ourselves are your servants for Jesus' sake. For God, who said, "Let there be light in the darkness," has made this light shine in our hearts so we could know the glory of God that is seen in the face of Jesus Christ.

We now have this light shining in our hearts, but we ourselves are like fragile clay jars containing this great treasure. This makes it clear that our great power is from God, not from ourselves.

2 Corinthians 4:1-7

Refrain:
Lord, let me see in the darkness.
Show me the light of life.

Psalm:
Praise the Lord, the God of Israel,
because he has visited and redeemed his people.
He has sent us a mighty Savior
from the royal line of his servant David,
just as he promised
through his holy prophets long ago.
Now we will be saved from our enemies
and from all who hate us.
He has been merciful to our ancestors
by remembering his sacred covenant—
the covenant he swore with an oath
to our ancestor Abraham.
We have been rescued from our enemies
so we can serve God without fear,
in holiness and righteousness
for as long as we live.

And you, my little son,
will be called the prophet of the Most High,
because you will prepare the way for the Lord.
You will tell his people how to find salvation
through forgiveness of their sins.
Because of God's tender mercy,

the morning light from heaven is about to break upon us,
to give light to those who sit in darkness and in the shadow of death,
    and to guide us to the path of peace.

Luke 1:68-79

Refrain:
Lord, let me see in the darkness.
    Show me the light of life.

The Lord's Prayer:
Our Father, who art in heaven,
Hallowed be thy name.
Thy kingdom come,
Thy will be done on earth,
As it is in heaven.
Give us this day our daily bread.
And forgive us our sins, as we forgive those who sin against us.
And lead us not into temptation, but deliver us from evil.
For thine is the kingdom, and the power, and the glory,
forever and ever.

Today's Prayer:
Your Word is clear that everything we have is a gift from you. Every
piece of technology, every bite of food we eat, every sip we take of our
favorite drink, and every minute we live: They are all gifts from you.
Help me on this Monday to see all these things as gifts. Help me not
miss them as I get back into the swing of things. Help me see my life
is filled with your gifts and is meant to be offered as a gift back to you
through how I live and use all the gifts you have given me. Help me to
make this day a gift to your world.

Concluding Prayer:
Guide us waking, O Lord, and guard us sleeping; that awake I may
watch with Christ and asleep I may rest in peace. *Amen.*

TUESDAY

DAWN PRAYER

Call to Prayer:
The whole earth is filled with awe at your wonders; where morning dawns, where evening fades, you call forth songs of joy.
Psalm 65:8 (NIV)

Invitation:
Come, let us sing for joy to the LORD;
    let us shout aloud to the Rock of our salvation.
Let us come before him with thanksgiving
    and extol him with music and song.
Psalm 95:1-2 (NIV)

Refrain:
Awake, my soul! Awake with music! I will awaken the dawn.

Reading:
After the Sabbath, at dawn on the first day of the week, Mary Magdalene and the other Mary went to look at the tomb.

There was a violent earthquake, for an angel of the Lord came down from heaven and, going to the tomb, rolled back the stone and sat on it. His appearance was like lightning, and his clothes were white as snow. The guards were so afraid of him that they shook and became like dead men.

The angel said to the women, "Do not be afraid, for I know that you are looking for Jesus, who was crucified. He is not here; he has risen, just as he said. Come and see the place where he lay. Then go quickly and tell his disciples: 'He has risen from the dead and is going ahead of you into Galilee. There you will see him.' Now I have told you."

So the women hurried away from the tomb, afraid yet filled with joy, and ran to tell his disciples. Suddenly Jesus met them. "Greetings," he said. They came to him, clasped his feet and worshiped him. Then Jesus said to them, "Do not be afraid. Go and tell my brothers to go to Galilee; there they will see me."
Matthew 28:1-10 (NIV)

Refrain:
Awake, my soul! Awake with music! I will awaken the dawn.

Psalm:
Will you not visit me?
The plant beside me feels your gentle dew.
Each blade of grass I see
From your deep earth its quickening moisture drew.

Will you not visit me?
The morning calls on me with cheering tone,
And every hill and tree
Has but one voice, the voice of you alone.

Come, for I need your love
More than the flower the dew or grass the rain;
Come like your Holy Dove,
And descending quickly bring me to life again.

Yes, you will visit me;
Neither plant nor tree you like so well
As when from sin set free,
Men's spirit comes in peace with you to dwell.

"Dawn"
by S. S. Wesley, 1800s
(author's adaptation)

Refrain:
Awake, my soul! Awake with music! I will awaken the dawn.

The Lord's Prayer:
Our Father, who art in heaven,
Hallowed be thy name.
Thy kingdom come,
Thy will be done on earth,
As it is in heaven.
Give us this day our daily bread.
And forgive us our sins, as we forgive those who sin against us.

And lead us not into temptation, but deliver us from evil.
For thine is the kingdom, and the power, and the glory,
forever and ever.

Today's Prayer:

You have taught us that every good and perfect gift comes from you,
because you are a good Father who loves his children. Forgive me
for thinking that all the good things I have are the work of my own
hands and help me to recognize the good things that happen today
as coming from you. Open my eyes and help me see through Jesus
Christ my Lord.

Concluding Prayer:

Ever-present God, you have brought me safely to the beginning of
this day. Give me grace to use it as a tool for the kingdom. Put me to
doing, put me to suffering. I surrender this day fully to your will, and
ask that you watch over me and empower me to avoid the potholes of
sin so that I may use this day to bring grace to the world and glory to
your name. *Amen.*

MORNING PRAYER

Call to Prayer:
I was glad when they said to me, "Let us go to the house of the LORD."

Psalm 122:1

Confession:
Almighty and most merciful Father,
I have made mistakes and strayed from your path like a lost sheep,
I have followed the lead of my own heart over your Spirit,
I have broken your law,
I have not done the things I knew you wanted me to do
and have done the things I knew you did not want me to do.

O Lord, have mercy upon me,
according to your promises in Jesus Christ.

And empower me, merciful Father,
to live a godly, righteous, and centered life from this point forward
to the glory of your holy name.

Invitation:
O Lord, open our lips
and our mouths shall show forth your praise.

Refrain:
Trust in the LORD with all your heart
    and lean not on your own understanding;
in all your ways submit to him,
    and he will make your paths straight.

Proverbs 3:5-6 (NIV)

Reading:
"Be careful, or your hearts will be weighed down with carousing, drunkenness, and the anxieties of life, and that day will close on you suddenly like a trap. For it will come on all those who live on the face of the whole earth. Be always on the watch, and pray that you may be

able to escape all that is about to happen, and that you may be able to stand before the Son of Man."

Each day Jesus was teaching at the temple, and each evening he went out to spend the night on the hill called the Mount of Olives, and all the people came early in the morning to hear him at the temple.

Luke 21:34-38 (NIV)

Refrain:

Trust in the LORD with all your heart
    and lean not on your own understanding;
in all your ways submit to him,
    and he will make your paths straight.

Proverbs 3:5-6 (NIV)

Psalm

Blessed is the one
    who does not walk in step with the wicked
or stand in the way that sinners take
    or sit in the company of mockers,
but whose delight is in the law of the LORD,
    and who meditates on his law day and night.
That person is like a tree planted by streams of water,
    which yields its fruit in season
and whose leaf does not wither—
    whatever they do prospers.
Not so the wicked!
They are like chaff
    that the wind blows away.
Therefore the wicked will not stand in the judgment,
    nor sinners in the assembly of the righteous.
For the LORD watches over the way of the righteous,
    but the way of the wicked leads to destruction.

Psalm 1 (NIV)

Refrain:

Trust in the LORD with all your heart
    and lean not on your own understanding;

in all your ways submit to him,
and he will make your paths straight.

Proverbs 3:5-6 (NIV)

The Lord's Prayer:
Our Father, who art in heaven,
Hallowed be thy name.
Thy kingdom come,
Thy will be done on earth,
As it is in heaven.
Give us this day our daily bread.
And forgive us our sins, as we forgive those who sin against us.
And lead us not into temptation, but deliver us from evil.
For thine is the kingdom, and the power, and the glory,
forever and ever.

Today's Prayer:
You have taught us that every good and perfect gift comes from you,
because you are a good Father who loves his children. Forgive me
for thinking that all the good things I have are the work of my own
hands and help me to recognize the good things that happen today
as coming from you. Open my eyes and help me see through Jesus
Christ my Lord.

Concluding Prayer:
O Lord, our heavenly Father, almighty and everlasting God, who has
brought me safely to the beginning of this day: Defend me with your
mighty power; empower me to not fall into sin or run into any kind
of danger but to do what is right in your eyes, through Jesus Christ
my Lord. *Amen.*

NOONDAY PRAYER

Call to Prayer:
Send me your light and your faithful care, let them lead me;
let them bring me to your holy mountain, to the place where you
dwell.

Psalm 43:3 (NIV)

Invitation:
The Lord has shown us his glory, let us come adore him.

Refrain:
O LORD, you have searched me, and know me.

Psalm 139:1 (ESV)

Psalm:
But I will sing of your strength,
    in the morning I will sing of your love;
for you are my fortress,
    my refuge in times of trouble.

You are my strength, I sing praise to you;
    you, God, are my fortress,
    my God on whom I can rely.

Psalm 59:16-17 (NIV)

Refrain:
O LORD, you have searched me, and know me.

Psalm 139:1 (ESV)

The Lord's Prayer:
Our Father, who art in heaven,
Hallowed be thy name.
Thy kingdom come,
Thy will be done on earth,
As it is in heaven.
Give us this day our daily bread.

And forgive us our sins, as we forgive those who sin against us.
And lead us not into temptation, but deliver us from evil.
For thine is the kingdom, and the power, and the glory,
forever and ever.

Today's Prayer:
You have taught us that every good and perfect gift comes from you, because you are a good Father who loves his children. Forgive me for thinking that all the good things I have are the work of my own hands and help me to recognize the good things that happen today as coming from you. Open my eyes and help me see through Jesus Christ my Lord.

Concluding Prayer:
Almighty Savior, who called Paul at noon to go and preach to the Gentiles: I pray that you would give light to my family and friends with the light of your grace and the brilliance of your mercy, so that all people may come and worship you. *Amen.*

AFTERNOON/AFTER SCHOOL PRAYER

Call to Prayer:
O God, come quickly to save us.
O Lord, make haste to help us.

Confession
Merciful Savior,
I have made it to the afternoon, but not perfectly.
Though my soul longs for obedience, I have done what I did not want to do.
Forgive me for these sins and those that I cannot remember.

Confess your specific sins to God.

In the name of Jesus Christ, I pray.

Invitation:
Bless the Lord who forgives all my sins;
His mercy endures forever.

Refrain:
As the sun sets and we have to turn on the lights,
Remind me that you call me to be a spiritual light
    in this dark world.
Help me to be the light you need me to be.

Reading:
When Jesus spoke again to the people, he said, "I am the light of the world. Whoever follows me will never walk in darkness, but will have the light of life."

The Pharisees challenged him, "Here you are, appearing as your own witness; your testimony is not valid."

Jesus answered, "Even if I testify on my own behalf, my testimony is valid, for I know where I came from and where I am going. But you have no idea where I come from or where I am going. You judge by human standards; I pass judgment on no one. But if I do judge, my decisions are true, because I am not alone. I stand with the Father, who sent me. In your own Law it is written that the testimony of two witnesses is true. I am one who testifies for myself; my other witness is the Father, who sent me."

Then they asked him, "Where is your father?"

"You do not know me or my Father," Jesus replied. "If you knew me, you would know my Father also." He spoke these words while teaching in the temple courts near the place where the offerings were put. Yet no one seized him, because his hour had not yet come.

John 8:12-20 (NIV)

Refrain:
As the sun sets and we have to turn on the lights,
Remind me that you call me to be a spiritual light
   in this dark world.
Help me to be the light you need me to be.

Psalm:
Light of life, angelic fire,
Love divine, yourself impart;
Every fainting soul inspire,
Shine in every drooping heart;
Every mournful sinner cheer,
Scatter all our guilty gloom,
Son of God, appear, appear!
To your human temples come.

Come in this accepted hour,
Bring your heavenly kingdom in;
Fill us with your glorious power,
Rooting out the seeds of sin;
Nothing more can we require,
We will want nothing less;
You be all our hearts' desire,
All our joy and all our peace.

"Light of Life Seraphic Fire"
by Charles Wesley, 1700s
(author's adaptation)

Refrain:
As the sun sets and we have to turn on the lights,
Remind me that you call me to be a spiritual light
     in this dark world.
Help me to be the light you need me to be.

The Lord's Prayer:
Our Father, who art in heaven,
Hallowed be thy name.
Thy kingdom come,
Thy will be done on earth,
As it is in heaven.
Give us this day our daily bread.
And forgive us our sins, as we forgive those who sin against us.
And lead us not into temptation, but deliver us from evil.
For thine is the kingdom, and the power, and the glory,
forever and ever.

Today's Prayer:
You have taught us that every good and perfect gift comes from you,
because you are a good Father who loves his children. Forgive me
for thinking that all the good things I have are the work of my own
hands and help me to recognize the good things that happen today
as coming from you. Open my eyes and help me see through Jesus
Christ my Lord.

Concluding Prayer:
O Lord, I began this day with you, and as I press forward to its end,
be with me. Guide me and let me avoid the ruts I have made that lead
to sin. Give me grace and peace for those around me as I use up my
energy. Show me how I might take these final hours and use them to
make earth look more like heaven. *Amen.*

END OF DAY PRAYER

Call to Prayer:
The Lord Almighty grant me a peaceful night and a perfect end.
from *The Book of Common Prayer*

Confession:
Almighty God, my heavenly Father:
I have sinned against you.
I sinned in my thoughts, and words, and actions,
and even in what I have left undone.
And no matter how I look at it, I know it was my own fault.
Because your Son, my Lord Jesus Christ, died for these very sins,
please forgive me,
and allow me to serve you
with a fresh start,
and use my life to bring you glory.

Invitation:
O God, make speed to save me.
O Lord, make haste to help me.

Refrain:
In peace I will lie down and sleep,
    for you alone, LORD,
    make me dwell in safety.

Psalm 4:8 (NIV)

Reading:
Whoever dwells in the shelter of the Most High
    will rest in the shadow of the Almighty.
I will say of the LORD, "He is my refuge and my fortress,
    my God, in whom I trust."
Surely he will save you
    from the fowler's snare
    and from the deadly pestilence.
He will cover you with his feathers,

and under his wings you will find refuge;
his faithfulness will be your shield and rampart.
You will not fear the terror of night,
    nor the arrow that flies by day,
    nor the pestilence that stalks in the darkness,
    nor the plague that destroys at midday.
A thousand may fall at your side,
    ten thousand at your right hand,
    but it will not come near you.
You will only observe with your eyes
    and see the punishment of the wicked.
If you say, "The LORD is my refuge,"
    and you make the Most High your dwelling,
    no harm will overtake you,
    no disaster will come near your tent.
For he will command his angels concerning you
    to guard you in all your ways;
    they will lift you up in their hands,
    so that you will not strike your foot against a stone.
You will tread on the lion and the cobra;
    you will trample the great lion and the serpent.
"Because he loves me," says the LORD, "I will rescue him;
    I will protect him, for he acknowledges my name.
He will call on me, and I will answer him;
    I will be with him in trouble,
    I will deliver him and honor him.
With long life I will satisfy him
    and show him my salvation."

Psalm 91 (NIV)

Refrain:
In peace I will lie down and sleep,
    for you alone, LORD,
    make me dwell in safety.

Psalm 4:8 (NIV)

Psalm:
Which of the monarchs of the earth

Can boast a guard like ours,
Encircled from our second birth
With all the heavenly powers?

Myriads of bright, angelic bands,
Sent by the King of Kings,
Rejoice to carry us in their hands,
And shade us with their wings.

Angels, wherever we go, attend
Our lives, whatever transpires;
With watchful care us they defend,
And evil turn aside.

Our lives those holy angels keep
From every hostile power;
And, unconcerned, we sweetly sleep,
As Adam in his garden bower.

And when our spirits we resign,
On outstretched wings they bear,
And lodge us in the arms divine,
And leave us ever there.

"Which of the Monarchs of the Earth"
by Charles Wesley, 1700s
(author's adaptation)

Refrain:
In peace I will lie down and sleep,
    for you alone, LORD,
        make me dwell in safety.

Psalm 4:8 (NIV)

The Lord's Prayer:
Our Father, who art in heaven,
Hallowed be thy name.
Thy kingdom come,
Thy will be done on earth,

As it is in heaven.
Give us this day our daily bread.
And forgive us our sins, as we forgive those who sin against us.
And lead us not into temptation, but deliver us from evil.
For thine is the kingdom, and the power, and the glory,
forever and ever.

Today's Prayer:

You have taught us that every good and perfect gift comes from you,
because you are a good Father who loves his children. Forgive me
for thinking that all the good things I have are the work of my own
hands and help me to recognize the good things that happen today
as coming from you. Open my eyes and help me see through Jesus
Christ my Lord.

Concluding Prayer:

I am finishing this day with you. From the beginning to the end you
were there listening to the cries of my heart and guiding my steps.
Now, I am in awe because I know that as I sleep your presence is
there with me. So, I ask that you will guard me as I sleep and guide
me when I wake, that awake I may live my life walking with you and
asleep I may rest in your holy peace. *Amen.*

MIDNIGHT PRAYER

Call to Prayer:
Blessed is the one
    who does not walk in step with the wicked
or stand in the way that sinners take
    or sit in the company of mockers,
but whose delight is in the law of the LORD,
    and who meditates on his law day and night.

Psalm 1:1-2 (NIV)

Invitation:
I call to you, LORD, come quickly to me;
    hear me when I call to you.
May my prayer be set before you like incense;
    may the lifting up of my hands be like the evening sacrifice.

Psalm 141:1-2 (NIV)

Refrain:
Lord, meet me in the stillness of this night;
    make light in the shadows for me.

Reading:
Immediately Jesus made the disciples get into the boat and go on ahead of him to the other side, while he dismissed the crowd. After he had dismissed them, he went up on a mountainside by himself to pray. Later that night, he was there alone, and the boat was already a considerable distance from land, buffeted by the waves because the wind was against it.

Shortly before dawn Jesus went out to them, walking on the lake. When the disciples saw him walking on the lake, they were terrified. "It's a ghost," they said, and cried out in fear.

But Jesus immediately said to them: "Take courage! It is I. Don't be afraid."

"Lord, if it's you," Peter replied, "tell me to come to you on the water."

"Come," he said.

Then Peter got down out of the boat, walked on the water and came toward Jesus. But when he saw the wind, he was afraid and, beginning to sink, cried out, "Lord, save me!"

Immediately Jesus reached out his hand and caught him. "You of little faith," he said, "why did you doubt?"

And when they climbed into the boat, the wind died down. Then those who were in the boat worshiped him, saying, "Truly you are the Son of God."

Matthew 14:22-33 (NIV)

Refrain:

Lord, meet me in the stillness of this night;
    make light in the shadows for me.

Psalm:

Dark is the night, and cold the wind is blowing,
Nearer and nearer comes the waves' roar;
Where shall I go, or fly for refuge?
Hide me, my Father, till the storm is over.

With his loving hand to guide, let the clouds above me roll,
And the waves in their fury dash around me.
I can brave the wildest storm, with his glory in my soul,
I can sing amidst the tempest—Praise the Lord!

Dark is the night, but cheering is the promise,
He will go with me over the troubled wave;
Safe he will lead me through the pathless waters,
Jesus, the Mighty One, and strong to save.

With his loving hand to guide, let the clouds above me roll,
And the waves in their fury dash around me.
I can brave the wildest storm, with his glory in my soul,
I can sing amidst the tempest—Praise the Lord!

Dark is the night, but look! The day is breaking,
Onward my bark, unfurl thy every sail,
Now at the helm I see my Father standing,

Soon will my anchor drop within the veil.

With his loving hand to guide, let the clouds above me roll,
And the waves in their fury dash around me.
I can brave the wildest storm, with his glory in my soul,
I can sing amidst the tempest—Praise the Lord!

> "Dark is the Night"
> by Fanny Crosby, 1800s
> (author's adaptation)

Refrain:
Lord, meet me in the stillness of this night;
  make light in the shadows for me.

The Lord's Prayer:
Our Father, who art in heaven,
Hallowed be thy name.
Thy kingdom come,
Thy will be done on earth,
As it is in heaven.
Give us this day our daily bread.
And forgive us our sins, as we forgive those who sin against us.
And lead us not into temptation, but deliver us from evil.
For thine is the kingdom, and the power, and the glory,
forever and ever.

Today's Prayer:
You have taught us that every good and perfect gift comes from you,
because you are a good Father who loves his children. Forgive me
for thinking that all the good things I have are the work of my own
hands and help me to recognize the good things that happen today
as coming from you. Open my eyes and help me see through Jesus
Christ my Lord.

Concluding Prayer:
May the Lord bless us and keep us and make his face to shine upon us
from this day forward and forever more. *Amen.*

WEDNESDAY

DAWN PRAYER

Call to Prayer:
How great is the goodness
    you have stored up for those who fear you.
You lavish it on those who come to you for protection,
    blessing them before the watching world.

Psalm 31:19

Invitation:
Join the song of creation! Lift your voice with the rocks and trees!
    Sing praises to your God for his love endures forever!

Refrain:
Sing praises to the LORD who reigns in Jerusalem.
    Tell the world about his unforgettable deeds.

Psalm 9:11

Reading:
During the night Jacob got up and took his two wives, his two servant wives, and his eleven sons and crossed the Jabbok River with them. After taking them to the other side, he sent over all his possessions.

This left Jacob all alone in the camp, and a man came and wrestled with him until the dawn began to break. When the man saw that he would not win the match, he touched Jacob's hip and wrenched it out of its socket. Then the man said, "Let me go, for the dawn is breaking!"

But Jacob said, "I will not let you go unless you bless me."

"What is your name?" the man asked.

He replied, "Jacob."

"Your name will no longer be Jacob," the man told him. "From now on you will be called Israel, because you have fought with God and with men and have won."

"Please tell me your name," Jacob said.

"Why do you want to know my name?" the man replied. Then he blessed Jacob there.

Jacob named the place Peniel (which means "face of God"), for he said, "I have seen God face to face, yet my life has been spared." The sun was rising as Jacob left Peniel, and he was limping because of the injury to his hip. (Even today the people of Israel don't eat the tendon near the hip socket because of what happened that night when the man strained the tendon of Jacob's hip.)

Genesis 32:22-32

Refrain:
Sing praises to the LORD who reigns in Jerusalem.
    Tell the world about his unforgettable deeds.

Psalm 9:11

Psalm:
Behold, the dawn is breaking,
In splendor is breaking,
When all the earth awaking
At Jesus' name shall bow;
When he, who once our sorrow bore,
Shall reign supreme from shore to shore,
Triumphant now and evermore
Our coming King of Glory.

Behold, the dawn is spreading,
In beauty is spreading;
The beams of love are shedding
The light of joy divine.
From Zion's tower the watchmen cry,
Rejoice! Rejoice! The time is nigh,
When we shall meet our Lord on high,
Our blessed King of Glory.

O dawn of rapture, telling
Where music is swelling
Within our Savior's dwelling
Above the stars that shine;
Where we shall breathe the fragrant air
Of yonder clime, serene and fair,
And all his faithful ones shall wear

A promised crown of glory.

"Behold the Dawn"
by Fanny Crosby, 1800s
(author's adaptation)

Refrain:

Sing praises to the LORD who reigns in Jerusalem.
    Tell the world about his unforgettable deeds.

Psalm 9:11

The Lord's Prayer:

Our Father, who art in heaven,
Hallowed be thy name.
Thy kingdom come,
Thy will be done on earth,
As it is in heaven.
Give us this day our daily bread.
And forgive us our sins, as we forgive those who sin against us.
And lead us not into temptation, but deliver us from evil.
For thine is the kingdom, and the power, and the glory,
forever and ever.

Today's Prayer:

You are the God of forever. Your love never fails. Your grace never
falters. As I come to the middle of my week, give me the gift of
perseverance. Give me the passion that helps me endure the difficult
and the mundane. Help me to reach beyond myself and echo your
consistency. May my life be an example of your foreverness today.

Concluding Prayer:

Most merciful God, you have allowed me to awaken to the beginning
of another day. Help me to start over with the breaking of the dawn.
Let me rise with the sun and walk forward in its light, ready to be the
light of the world today. Free me from the chains of yesterday and let
me not be distracted by the phantom of tomorrow. Walk with me into
the beginning of another day filled with possibility. *Amen.*

MORNING PRAYER

Call to Prayer:
From atoms to galaxies, all your works sing your praise.

Confession:
Turn to me and have mercy,
    for I am alone and in deep distress.
My problems go from bad to worse.
    Oh, save me from them all!
Feel my pain and see my trouble.
    Forgive all my sins.

Psalm 25:16-18

Invitation:
Bring me to the waters of life that I may drink in your mercy.

Refrain:
I cried out to the LORD in my great trouble,
    and he answered me.
I called to you from the land of the dead,
    and LORD, you heard me!

Jonah 2:2

Reading:
"If only the LORD had killed us back in Egypt," they moaned. "There we sat around pots filled with meat and ate all the bread we wanted. But now you have brought us into this wilderness to starve us all to death."

Then the LORD said to Moses, "Look, I'm going to rain down food from heaven for you. Each day the people can go out and pick up as much food as they need for that day. I will test them in this to see whether or not they will follow my instructions. On the sixth day they will gather food, and when they prepare it, there will be twice as much as usual."

So Moses and Aaron said to all the people of Israel, "By evening you will realize it was the LORD who brought you out of the land of

Egypt. In the morning you will see the glory of the LORD, because
he has heard your complaints, which are against him, not against us.
What have we done that you should complain about us?" Then Moses
added, "The LORD will give you meat to eat in the evening and bread
to satisfy you in the morning, for he has heard all your complaints
against him. What have we done? Yes, your complaints are against the
LORD, not against us."

Exodus 16:3-8

Refrain:
I cried out to the LORD in my great trouble,
    and he answered me.
I called to you from the land of the dead,
    and LORD, you heard me!

Jonah 2:2

Psalm
Every morning mercies new
Fall as fresh as morning dew;
Every morning let us pay
Tribute with the early day;
For your mercies, Lord, are sure;
Your compassion does endure.

Still the greatness of your love
Daily does our sins remove;
Daily, far as east from west,
Lifts the burden from the chest;
Gives freely, to those who pray,
Strength to stand in evil day.

Let our prayers each morning prevail,
That these gifts may never fail;
And, as we confess the sin
And the tempter's power within,
Feed us with the Bread of Life,
Equip us for our daily strife.

As the morning light returns,
As the sun with splendor burns,
Teach us still to turn to you,
Ever blessed Trinity,
With our hands our hearts to raise,
In unfailing prayer and praise.

"Every Morning Mercies New"
by Greville Phillimore, 1800s
(author's adaptation)

Refrain:
I cried out to the LORD in my great trouble,
     and he answered me.
I called to you from the land of the dead,
     and LORD, you heard me!

Jonah 2:2

The Lord's Prayer:
Our Father, who art in heaven,
Hallowed be thy name.
Thy kingdom come,
Thy will be done on earth,
As it is in heaven.
Give us this day our daily bread.
And forgive us our sins, as we forgive those who sin against us.
And lead us not into temptation, but deliver us from evil.
For thine is the kingdom, and the power, and the glory,
forever and ever.

Today's Prayer:
You are the God of forever. Your love never fails. Your grace never
falters. As I come to the middle of my week, give me the gift of
perseverance. Give me the passion that helps me endure the difficult
and the mundane. Help me to reach beyond myself and echo your
consistency. May my life be an example of your foreverness today.

Concluding Prayer:
Heavenly Father, we begin another day together, and I ask that you

help me to begin this day well. Let me to see the opportunities you place before me, and guard me from all that might lead me astray. Fill me with your Spirit that I may stretch beyond my own abilities and follow you in holiness, through Jesus Christ my Lord. *Amen.*

NOONDAY PRAYER

Call to Prayer:
Shine down on me from above. Send me your wisdom and wash over me with mercy.

Invitation:
I pray to you, O LORD, my rock.
    Do not turn a deaf ear to me.
For if you are silent,
    I might as well give up and die.
Listen to my prayer for mercy
    as I cry out to you for help,
    as I lift my hands toward your holy sanctuary.

Psalm 28:1-2

Refrain:
In the middle of the day I cry out to you. Shine in me like the noonday sun.

Psalm:
From noon of joy to night of doubt
our feelings come and go;
our best estate is tossed about
in ceaseless ebb and flow;
no mood or feeling, form of thought,
is constant for a day,
but you, O Lord, you change not;
you are the same always.

"From Noon of Joy to Night of Doubt"
by John Campbell Shairp, 1800s
(author's adaptation)

Refrain:
In the middle of the day I cry out to you. Shine in me like the noonday sun.

The Lord's Prayer:
Our Father, who art in heaven,
Hallowed be thy name.
Thy kingdom come,
Thy will be done on earth,
As it is in heaven.
Give us this day our daily bread.
And forgive us our sins, as we forgive those who sin against us.
And lead us not into temptation, but deliver us from evil.
For thine is the kingdom, and the power, and the glory,
forever and ever.

Today's Prayer:
You are the God of forever. Your love never fails. Your grace never falters. As I come to the middle of my week, give me the gift of perseverance. Give me the passion that helps me endure the difficult and the mundane. Help me to reach beyond myself and echo your consistency. May my life be an example of your foreverness today.

Concluding Prayer:
Almighty Savior, who stopped the sun in the middle of the sky for Joshua, be with me, I pray. Give me the power to concentrate after lunch and make these hours so productive that it feels like you stopped the sun in the sky for me. As I continue into the rest of this day, may I bring the light of your grace to all the situations ahead of me that people would see you as bright as the noonday sun in me and give glory to your name. *Amen.*

AFTERNOON/AFTER SCHOOL PRAYER

Call to Prayer:
Come, let us tell of the LORD's greatness;
> let us exalt his name together.

> Psalm 34:3

Confession:
Almighty and most merciful God,
I find myself in need of forgiveness again this afternoon.
I have ignored people in need;
I have wounded people you created;
I have sinned by my words, actions, and inaction.
Forgive me.
Free me.
So that I can joyfully serve you with the rest of this day.

Invitation:
I prayed to the LORD, and he answered me.
> He freed me from all my fears.
Those who look to him for help will be radiant with joy;
> no shadow of shame will darken their faces.
In my desperation I prayed, and the LORD listened;
> he saved me from all my troubles.
For the angel of the LORD is a guard;
> he surrounds and defends all who fear him.

> Psalm 34:4-7

Refrain:
I will give thanks to the LORD because of his righteousness;
> I will sing the praises of the name of the LORD Most High.

> Psalm 7:17 (NIV)

Reading:
Peter and John went to the Temple one afternoon to take part in the three o'clock prayer service. As they approached the Temple, a man lame from birth was being carried in. Each day he was put beside the

Temple gate, the one called the Beautiful Gate, so he could beg from the people going into the Temple. When he saw Peter and John about the enter, he asked them for some money.

Peter and John looked at him intently, and Peter said, "Look at us!"

The lame man looked at them eagerly, expecting some money. But Peter said, "I don't have any silver or gold for you. But I'll give you what I have. In the name of Jesus Christ the Nazarene, get up and walk!"

Then Peter took the lame man by the right hand and helped him up. And as he did, the man's feet and ankles were instantly healed and strengthened. He jumped up, stood on his feet, and began to walk! Then, walking, leaping, and praising God, he went into the Temple with them.

All the people saw him walking and heard him praising God. When they realized he was the lame beggar they had seen so often at the Beautiful Gate, they were absolutely astounded! They all rushed out in amazement to Solomon's Colonnade, where the man was holding tightly to Peter and John.

Acts 3:1-11

Refrain:
I will give thanks to the LORD because of his righteousness;
>   I will sing the praises of the name of the LORD Most High.

Psalm 7:17 (NIV)

Psalm:
A giddy lamb one afternoon
>   Had from the fold departed.
The tender shepherd missed it soon
>   And sought it broken hearted.
Not all the flock that shared his love
>   Could from the search delay him,
Nor clouds of midnight darkness move,
>   Nor fear of suffering stay him.

But night and day he went his way
>   In sorrow till he found it,

And when he saw it fainting lie,
    He clasped his arms around it.
Then safely folded to his breast
    From every ill to save it,
He brought it to his home of rest
    And pitied and forgave it.

And thus the Savior will receive
    The little ones who fear him.
Their pains remove, their sins forgive,
    And draw them gently near him.

"The Strayed Lamb"
Author Unknown, 1856
(author's adaptation)

Refrain:
I will give thanks to the LORD because of his righteousness;
    I will sing the praises of the name of the LORD Most High.

Psalm 7:17 (NIV)

The Lord's Prayer:
Our Father, who art in heaven,
Hallowed be thy name.
Thy kingdom come,
Thy will be done on earth,
As it is in heaven.
Give us this day our daily bread.
And forgive us our sins, as we forgive those who sin against us.
And lead us not into temptation, but deliver us from evil.
For thine is the kingdom, and the power, and the glory,
forever and ever.

Today's Prayer:
You are the God of forever. Your love never fails. Your grace never
falters. As I come to the middle of my week, give me the gift of
perseverance. Give me the passion that helps me endure the difficult
and the mundane. Help me to reach beyond myself and echo your
consistency. May my life be an example of your foreverness today.

Concluding Prayer:

Almighty Creator, merciful Redeemer, as the sun sinks lower in the sky I pray that you would give me the gift of perseverance. Let me endure to the end with integrity and honor. Give me light to see my way along the path of righteousness. Guide my steps to follow you, fill my mouth with your words, and use my hands to comfort your people and fight for justice. *Amen.*

END OF DAY PRAYER

Call to Prayer:
May the Lord Almighty grant me and those I love a peaceful night
and a perfect end.

from The Book of Common Prayer

Confession:
I need your mercy. I have sinned.
> Though you know my thoughts, and you have seen all my deeds,
> I confess them to you now.

Reflect on your day. Name your sins to God.

Forgive me, most merciful God.
> Relieve the burden of my sin
> And guide me tomorrow along the paths of righteousness.

Invitation:

Our help is from the LORD,
> who made heaven and earth.

Psalm 124:8

Refrain:
You can go to bed without fear;
> you will lie down and sleep soundly.
You need not be afraid of sudden disaster
> or the destruction that comes upon the wicked,
For the LORD is your security.
> He will keep your foot from being caught in a trap.

Proverbs 3:24-26

Reading:
There was a man named Nicodemus, a Jewish religious leader who
was a Pharisee. After dark one evening, he came to speak with Jesus.
"Rabbi," he said, "we all know that God has sent you to teach us. Your

miraculous signs are evidence that God is with you."

Jesus replied, "I tell you the truth, unless you are born again, you cannot see the kingdom of God."

"What do you mean?" exclaimed Nicodemus. "How can an old man go back into his mother's womb and be born again?"

Jesus replied, "I assure you, no one can enter the kingdom of God without being born of water and the Spirit. Humans can reproduce only human life, but the Holy Spirit gives birth to spiritual life. So don't be surprised when I say, 'You must be born again.' The wind blows wherever it wants. Just as you can hear the wind but can't tell where it comes from or where it is going, so you can't explain how people are born of the Spirit."

"How are these things possible?" Nicodemus asked.

Jesus replied, "You are a respected Jewish teacher, and yet you don't understand these things? I assure you, we tell you what we know and have seen, and yet you won't believe our testimony. But if you don't believe me when I tell you about earthly things, how can you possibly believe if I tell you about heavenly things? No one has ever gone to heaven and returned. But the Son of Man has come down from heaven. And as Moses lifted up the bronze snake on a pole in the wilderness, so the Son of Man must be lifted up, so that everyone who believes in him will have eternal life.

"For God loved the world so much that he gave his one and only Son, so that everyone who believes in him will not perish but have eternal life. God sent his Son into the world not to judge the world, but to save the world through him."

John 3:1-17

Refrain:
You can go to bed without fear;
> you will lie down and sleep soundly.
You need not be afraid of sudden disaster
> or the destruction that comes upon the wicked,
For the LORD is your security.
> He will keep your foot from being caught in a trap.

Proverbs 3:24-26

Psalm:

Before the ending of the day,
Creator of the world, we pray,
That with your usual favor
Wouldst be our guard and keeper.

From all ill dreams defend our eyes,
From nightly fears and fantasies;
Tread under foot our ghostly foe,
That no pollution we may know.

O Father, we ask this be done,
Through Jesus Christ your only Son,
Who, with the Holy Ghost and thee,
Does live and reign eternally.

"Before the Ending of the Day"
by Saint Ambrose, 340-397
(author's adaptation)

Refrain:

You can go to bed without fear;
    you will lie down and sleep soundly.
You need not be afraid of sudden disaster
    or the destruction that comes upon the wicked,
For the LORD is your security.
    He will keep your foot from being caught in a trap.

Proverbs 3:24-26

The Lord's Prayer:

Our Father, who art in heaven,
Hallowed be thy name.
Thy kingdom come,
Thy will be done on earth,
As it is in heaven.
Give us this day our daily bread.
And forgive us our sins, as we forgive those who sin against us.
And lead us not into temptation, but deliver us from evil.
For thine is the kingdom, and the power, and the glory,

forever and ever.

Today's Prayer:
You are the God of forever. Your love never fails. Your grace never falters. As I come to the middle of my week, give me the gift of perseverance. Give me the passion that helps me endure the difficult and the mundane. Help me to reach beyond myself and echo your consistency. May my life be an example of your foreverness today.

Concluding Prayer:
As I close my shades on another day, I pray that you would keep me through the night and bring me through it to a glorious morning. *Amen.*

MIDNIGHT PRAYER

Call to Prayer:

Then I will rejoice in the LORD.
    I will be glad because he rescues me.

Psalm 35:9

Invitation:

I call to you, LORD, come quickly to me;
    hear me when I call to you.
May my prayer be set before you like incense;
    may the lifting up of my hands be like the evening sacrifice.

Psalm 141:1-2 (NIV)

Refrain:

Trust in the LORD and do good.
    Then you will live safely in the land and prosper.

Psalm 37:3

Reading:

Around midnight Paul and Silas were praying and singing hymns to God, and the other prisoners were listening. Suddenly, there was a massive earthquake, and the prison was shaken to its foundations. All the doors immediately flew open, and the chains of every prisoner fell off! The jailer woke up to see the prison doors wide open. He assumed the prisoners had escaped, so he drew his sword to kill himself. But Paul shouted to him, "Stop! Don't kill yourself! We are all here!"

The jailer called for lights and ran to the dungeon and fell down trembling before Paul and Silas. Then he brought them out and asked, "Sirs, what must I do to be saved?"

They replied, "Believe in the Lord Jesus and you will be saved, along with everyone in your household." And they shared the word of the Lord with him and with all who lived in his household. Even at that hour of the night, the jailer cared for them and washed their wounds. Then he and everyone in his household were immediately baptized.

He brought them into his house and set a meal before them, and he and his entire household rejoiced because they all believed in God.

The next morning the city officials sent the police to tell the jailer, "Let those men go!" So the jailer told Paul, "The city officials have said you and Silas are free to leave. Go in peace."

Acts 16:25-36

Refrain:
Trust in the LORD and do good.
Then you will live safely in the land and prosper.

Psalm 37:3

Psalm:
Church of Christ, your Lord is calling;
Open your eyes, behold and see,
Precious souls, in chains of bondage,
For help from you they do now plead.
Up and work for those that perish,
Haste, the time will soon be over;
Fold your arms of love around them,
Church of Christ, O sleep no more.

Lo, again your Lord is calling;
Preach the Word, its truth proclaim;
Lift your voice and, like a trumpet,
Sound aloud our God's name.
Foreboding clouds are in the distance,
Billows foam, and surges roar,
Dark and wild the night is coming,
Church of Christ, O sleep no more.

Still again your Lord is calling;
Take the lamp that once he gave;
Let its beams of matchless glory
Shine afar the lost to save.
Do his will and do it quickly,
For the time will soon be over;
He may come when least expected,

Church of Christ, O sleep no more.

"Church of Christ, O Sleep No More"
by Fanny Crosby, 1800s
(author's adaptation)

Refrain:
Trust in the LORD and do good.
Then you will live safely in the land and prosper.

Psalm 37:3

The Lord's Prayer:
Our Father, who art in heaven,
Hallowed be thy name.
Thy kingdom come,
Thy will be done on earth,
As it is in heaven.
Give us this day our daily bread.
And forgive us our sins, as we forgive those who sin against us.
And lead us not into temptation, but deliver us from evil.
For thine is the kingdom, and the power, and the glory,
forever and ever.

Today's Prayer:
You are the God of forever. Your love never fails. Your grace never
falters. As I come to the middle of my week, give me the gift of
perseverance. Give me the passion that helps me endure the difficult
and the mundane. Help me to reach beyond myself and echo your
consistency. May my life be an example of your foreverness today.

Concluding Prayer:
May the God of light shine upon me and grant me a life of peace for
all my days ahead. As I turn to sleep once more, recharge me and
grant me a peaceful night. *Amen.*

THURSDAY

DAWN PRAYER

Call to Prayer:

How can I express with words the glory of a God who created the universe,

> whose voice has the power to call life forth from death,
> whose love stretches beyond torture and the grave,
> whose grace covers all my brokenness?

Invitation:

And the LORD came and called as before, "Samuel! Samuel!"
And Samuel replied, "Speak, your servant is listening."

1 Samuel 3:10

Refrain:

I said to myself, "I will watch what I do
> and not sin in what I say.
I will hold my tongue
> when the ungodly are around me."

Psalm 39:1

Reading:

Dear brothers and sisters, not many of you should become teachers in the church, for we who teach will be judged more strictly. Indeed, we all make many mistakes. For if we could control our tongues, we would be perfect and could also control ourselves in every other way.

We can make a large horse go wherever we want by means of a small bit in its mouth. And a small rudder makes a huge ship turn wherever the pilot chooses to go, even though the winds are strong. In the same way, the tongue is a small thing that makes grand speeches.

But a tiny spark can set a great forest on fire. And among all the parts of the body, the tongue is a flame of fire. It is a whole world of wickedness, corrupting your entire body. It can set your whole life on fire, for it is set on fire by hell itself.

People can tame all kinds of animals, birds, reptiles, and fish, but no one can tame the tongue. It is restless and evil, full of deadly poison. Sometimes it praises our Lord and Father, and sometimes it curses those who have been made in the image of God. And so blessing and cursing come pouring out of the same mouth. Surely, my brothers and sisters, this is not right! Does a spring of water bubble out with both fresh water and bitter water?

James 3:1-11

Refrain:
I said to myself, "I will watch what I do
    and not sin in what I say.
I will hold my tongue
    when the ungodly are around me."

Psalm 39:1

Psalm:
With all my powers of heart and tongue,
I'll praise my Maker in my song;
Angels shall hear the notes I raise,
Approve the song, and join the praise.
The angels make your church their care;
They'll witness my devotion there.
I'll sing your truth and mercy, Lord;
I'll sing the wonders of your Word.

I cried to you when troubles rose;
You heard me and subdued my foes;
My fears dispersed through your control,
And strength diffused through all my soul.
Grace will complete what grace begins,
To save from sorrows and from sins;
Work that your wisdom undertakes
Eternal mercy ne'er forsakes.

"With All My Powers of Heart and Tongue"
by Isaac Watts, 1740
(author's adaptation)

Refrain:

I said to myself, "I will watch what I do
  and not sin in what I say.
I will hold my tongue
  when the ungodly are around me."

Psalm 39:1

The Lord's Prayer:

Our Father, who art in heaven,
Hallowed be thy name.
Thy kingdom come,
Thy will be done on earth,
As it is in heaven.
Give us this day our daily bread.
And forgive us our sins, as we forgive those who sin against us.
And lead us not into temptation, but deliver us from evil.
For thine is the kingdom, and the power, and the glory,
forever and ever.

Today's Prayer:

Everything I have ever seen, everything I have ever read, every inch
of creation that ever existed was created by you. All of it is yours.
From the sunrise to the greatest mountains to the plankton in the
seas, it is all yours. I sit surrounded by your creation, knowing that
just like the sand and the sea, I am created by you. I am yours. Today,
help me to remember that. Help me rest in the knowledge that I have
been created by a loving God.

Concluding Prayer:

As I begin this day, help me to be careful with how I use my words.
Help me to use them to echo your own words that bring life,
offer grace, and create glorious things from nothing. Give me the
supernatural power to stop before I wound with my words. May my
words be like a spring of fresh water welling up in my world wherever
I go today. *Amen.*

MORNING PRAYER

Call to Prayer:
Then Jesus said, "Come to me, all of you who are weary and carry
heavy burdens, and I will give you rest.

Matthew 11:28

Confession:
Merciful God, I begin this day asking for your forgiveness.
Forgive me for the sinful thoughts that filled my mind last night and
yesterday.
Forgive me for not turning away from sin even when I knew what I
was doing.
Forgive me for the wounds I inflicted on myself
    and on others
    even my friends.
Wipe away the stain of my sin.
Not because I deserve it, because I don't.
Forgive me because of your Son, my Savior Jesus Christ,
And cleanse me from all unrighteousness.

Invitation:
I am open. You are here. I am listening.
Come, Holy Spirit.

Refrain:
Don't worry about the wicked or envy those who do wrong.

Psalm 37:1

Reading:
That is why I tell you not to worry about everyday life—whether
you have enough food and drink, or enough clothes to wear. Isn't
life more than food, and your body more than clothing? Look at the
birds. They don't plant or harvest or store food in barns, for your
heavenly Father feeds them. And aren't you far more valuable to him
than they are? Can all your worries add a single moment to your life?

    And why worry about your clothing? Look at the lilies of the field and how they grow. They don't work or make their clothing, yet Solomon in all his glory was not dressed as beautifully as they are. And if God cares so wonderfully for wildflowers that are here today and thrown into the fire tomorrow, he will certainly care for you. Why do you have so little faith?

So don't worry about these things, saying, "What will we eat? What will we drink? What will we wear?" These things dominate the thoughts of unbelievers, but your heavenly Father already knows all your needs. Seek the kingdom of God above all else, and live righteously, and he will give you everything you need.

So don't worry about tomorrow, for tomorrow will bring its own worries. Today's trouble is enough for today.

Matthew 6:25-34

Refrain:

Don't worry about the wicked or envy those who do wrong.

Psalm 37:1

Psalm

I cry out to the LORD;
    I plead for the LORD's mercy.
I pour out my complaints before him
    and tell him all my troubles.
When I am overwhelmed,
    you alone know the way I should turn.
Wherever I go,
    my enemies have set traps for me.
I look for someone to come and help me,
    but no one gives me a passing thought!
No one will help me;
    no one cares a bit what happens to me.
Then I pray to you, O LORD.
    I say, "You are my place of refuge.
    You are all I really want in life.
Hear my cry,
    for I am very low.
Rescue me from my persecutors,
    for they are too strong for me.

Bring me out of prison
    so I can thank you.
The godly will crowd around me,
    for you are good to me."

Psalm 142

Refrain:

Don't worry about the wicked or envy those who do wrong.

Psalm 37:1

The Lord's Prayer:

Our Father, who art in heaven,
Hallowed be thy name.
Thy kingdom come,
Thy will be done on earth,
As it is in heaven.
Give us this day our daily bread.
And forgive us our sins, as we forgive those who sin against us.
And lead us not into temptation, but deliver us from evil.
For thine is the kingdom, and the power, and the glory,
forever and ever.

Today's Prayer:

Everything I have ever seen, everything I have ever read, every inch of creation that ever existed was created by you. All of it is yours. From the sunrise to the greatest mountains to the plankton in the seas, it is all yours. I sit surrounded by your creation, knowing that just like the sand and the sea, I am created by you. I am yours. Today, help me to remember that. Help me rest in the knowledge that I have been created by a loving God.

Concluding Prayer:

As I start this day, give me the grace to be present wherever I find myself. Give me strength to not spend my day running ahead and worrying about what may be in my future. Let my mind stay in the here and now and give my heart peace right where I am. Let me not be anxious about the future but centered for the present. *Amen.*

NOONDAY PRAYER

Call to Prayer:
Then the righteous will shine like the sun in their Father's kingdom.
Anyone with ears to hear should listen and understand!

Matthew 13:43

Invitation:
God, you sent your only Son to earth
    to teach and live and die and be raised back to life
    because you love us,
    because you love me.
Do not turn a deaf ear or a blind eye;
    look on me with your grace-filled eyes;
    listen to me like a loving Father.
Lord, in your mercy, hear my prayer.

Refrain:
For you bless the godly, O LORD;
    you surround them with your shield of love.

Psalm 5:12

Psalm:
As the heart when noon is burning
Pants for springs where waters burst,
So for God my soul is yearning,
For the living God I thirst.
When shall I, a wanderer here,
In your presence, Lord, appear?
Daily by my enemies mocked,
Tears they for my food provided.

If fond memories seek to borrow
Comfort from my former years,
These but stir anew my sorrow,
Open every spout of tears.
To your gates with singing,

The crowd I often was leading,
Who with joy and praise adore you,
Continue to rest before you.

Why are you discouraged and fearful?
O my soul, why so dismayed?
Hope in God, and eyes now tearful
Yet will see his present aid.
Down, O God, my heart is cast,
Till I think of mercies past;
Then to you, my spirit weary
Turns as from a desert dreary.

As your waterfalls resounding,
Deep is calling to deep.
Over me, your all-surrounding
Waves and clouds wildly sweep.
Yet the Lord will bless my days,
I, his loving-kindness praise;
And his song, at midnight given,
Be my prayer to God in heaven.

Why uneasiness within me!
Why do you, my soul, feel down!
Hope in God, I yet will praise him,
Who with joy my life will crown.
He, my God, whose wondrous grace
Is the help that cheers my face,
Comforts me, when tears are blinding,
As the heart cool waters finding.

"As the Heart When Noon Is Burning"
by Edwin A. Collier, 1898
(author's adaptation)

Refrain:
For you bless the godly, O LORD;
    you surround them with your shield of love.

Psalm 5:12

The Lord's Prayer:
Our Father, who art in heaven,
Hallowed be thy name.
Thy kingdom come,
Thy will be done on earth,
As it is in heaven.
Give us this day our daily bread.
And forgive us our sins, as we forgive those who sin against us.
And lead us not into temptation, but deliver us from evil.
For thine is the kingdom, and the power, and the glory,
forever and ever.

Today's Prayer:
Everything I have ever seen, everything I have ever read, every inch of creation that ever existed was created by you. All of it is yours. From the sunrise to the greatest mountains to the plankton in the seas, it is all yours. I sit surrounded by your creation, knowing that just like the sand and the sea, I am created by you. I am yours. Today, help me to remember that. Help me rest in the knowledge that I have been created by a loving God.

Concluding Prayer:
Everlasting God, who has brought me again to the middle of my day, you know where I am. You know what I need even if I do not. Can you refresh my heart with your springs of life? Will you help me stay aware of your presence as I continue with all that lies ahead? I know that I can go through the rest of this day at ease when I know that you are with me. Give me the grace of being able to sense your presence and the boldness to live accordingly. *Amen.*

AFTERNOON/AFTER SCHOOL PRAYER

Call to Prayer:

I will praise your mighty deeds, O Sovereign LORD.
I will tell everyone that you alone are just.

Psalm 71:16

Confession

Have mercy on me, O God,
because of your unfailing love.
Because of your great compassion,
blot out the stain of my sins.
Wash me clean from my guilt.
Purify me from my sin.
For I recognize my rebellion;
it haunts me day and night.
Against you, and you alone, have I sinned;
I have done what is evil in your sight.
You will be proved right in what you say,
and your judgment against me is just.

Psalm 51:1-4

Invitation:

In this moment, I need to know that you're listening.
That you are hearing the cries of my heart.
I know you have entered my open heart before.
You have guided my willing hands and feet and put them to your tasks.
You have spoken to my listening heart.
Hear my cries.
I am open. I am willing. I am listening.
Again.

Refrain:

Be near to me, O God.
Speak your words of light and truth.

Reading:

"Don't let your hearts be troubled. Trust in God, and trust also in me. There is more than enough room in my Father's home. If this were not so, would I have told you that I am going to prepare a place for you? When everything is ready, I will come and get you, so that you will always be with me where I am. And you know the way to where I am going."

"No, we don't know, Lord," Thomas said. "We have no idea where you are going, so how can we know the way?"

Jesus told him, "I am the way, the truth, and the life. No one can come to the Father except through me. If you had really known me, you would know who my Father is. From now on, you do know him and have seen him!"

Philip said, "Lord, show us the Father, and we will be satisfied."

Jesus replied, "Have I been with you all this time, Philip, and yet you still don't know who I am? Anyone who has seen me has seen the Father! So why are you asking me to show him to you? Don't you believe that I am in the Father and the Father is in me? The words I speak are not my own, but my Father who lives in me does his work through me. Just believe that I am in the Father and the Father is in me. Or at least believe because of the work you have seen me do.

"I tell you the truth, anyone who believes in me will do the same works I have done, and even greater works, because I am going to be with the Father."

John 14:1-12

Refrain:

Be near to me, O God.
Speak your words of light and truth.

Psalm:

Talk with us, Lord, yourself reveal,
While here over earth we roam;
Speak to our hearts, and let us feel
The kindling of your love.

With you conversing, we forget
All time and toil and care;

Labor is rest, and pain is sweet,
If you, my God, are here.

You call me to seek your face,
It is all I wish to seek;
To hear the whispers of your grace,
And hear you in me speak.

Let this my every hour employ,
Till I your glory see,
Enter into my Master's joy,
And find my heaven in thee.

"Talk with Us, Lord, Thyself Reveal"
by Charles Wesley, 1740
(author's adaptation)

Refrain:
Be near to me, O God.
Speak your words of light and truth.

The Lord's Prayer:
Our Father, who art in heaven,
Hallowed be thy name.
Thy kingdom come,
Thy will be done on earth,
As it is in heaven.
Give us this day our daily bread.
And forgive us our sins, as we forgive those who sin against us.
And lead us not into temptation, but deliver us from evil.
For thine is the kingdom, and the power, and the glory,
forever and ever.

Today's Prayer:
Everything I have ever seen, everything I have ever read, every inch
of creation that ever existed was created by you. All of it is yours.
From the sunrise to the greatest mountains to the plankton in the
seas, it is all yours. I sit surrounded by your creation, knowing that
just like the sand and the sea, I am created by you. I am yours. Today,

help me to remember that. Help me rest in the knowledge that I have been created by a loving God.

Concluding Prayer:
Your words are the source of life. Though sometimes I'm not quite sure if I am hearing them. As I continue forward, I pray that the closeness of your presence would help me to hear and recognize your voice speaking to my heart. May I hear and obey your words so that the rest of this day I can walk along your path acting as your hands and feet to those I meet along the way. *Amen.*

END OF DAY PRAYER

Call to Prayer:
May the Lord Almighty grant me and those I love a peaceful night
and a perfect end.

from The Book of Common Prayer

Confession:
It has been another day of sin. And though you know them all, I take
the time to confess them to you.

> *Think through your day.*
> *Think about the morning.*
> *Think about the afternoon.*
> *Think about the evening and night.*
> *Confess the sins you have committed during each specific*
> *timeframe.*

Forgive me for these sins.
> Free me from their guilt and shame.
> Free me so that I can be joyfully obedient
For the sake of your Son Jesus Christ, my Savior.

Invitation:
You are right here among us, LORD.
> We are known as your people.
> Please don't abandon us now!

Jeremiah 14:9b

Refrain:
May this night be one of peace and may my bed be one of rest.
Fill my dreams with thoughts of you
And wake me ready for another day.

Reading:
Meanwhile, the boy Samuel served the LORD by assisting Eli. Now in
those days messages from the LORD were very rare, and visions were

quite uncommon.

One night Eli, who was almost blind by now, had gone to bed. The lamp of God had not yet gone out, and Samuel was sleeping in the Tabernacle near the Ark of God. Suddenly the LORD called out, "Samuel!"

"Yes?" Samuel replied. "What is it?" He got up and ran to Eli. "Here I am. Did you call me?"

"I didn't call you," Eli replied. "Go back to bed." So he did. Then the LORD called out again, "Samuel!"

Again Samuel got up and went to Eli. "Here I am. Did you call me?"

"I didn't call you, my son," Eli said. "Go back to bed."

Samuel did not yet know the LORD because he had never had a message from the LORD before. So the LORD called a third time, and once more Samuel got up and went to Eli. "Here I am. Did you call me?"

Then Eli realized it was the LORD who was calling the boy. So he said to Samuel, "Go and lie down again, and if someone calls again, say, 'Speak, LORD, your servant is listening.'" So Samuel went back to bed.

And the LORD came and called as before, "Samuel! Samuel!"

And Samuel replied, "Speak, your servant is listening."

Then the LORD said to Samuel, "I am about to do a shocking thing in Israel. I am going to carry out all my threats against Eli and his family, from beginning to end. I have warned him that judgment is coming upon his family forever, because his sons are blaspheming God and he hasn't disciplined them. So I have vowed that the sins of Eli and his sons will never be forgiven by sacrifices or offerings."

1 Samuel 3:1-14

Refrain:

May this night be one of peace and may my bed be one of rest.
Fill my dreams with thoughts of you
And wake me ready for another day.

Psalm:

All praise to You, my God, this night,
For all the blessings of the light.

Keep me, O keep me, King of Kings,
Beneath the shelter of your wings.

Forgive me, Lord, for this I pray,
The wrong that I have done this day.
May peace with God and neighbor be,
Before I sleep restored to me.

Lord, may I be at rest in you
And sweetly sleep the whole night through.
Refresh my strength, for your own sake,
So I may serve you when I wake.

Praise God, from whom all blessings flow;
Praise him all creatures here below;
Praise him above, ye heavenly host;
Praise Father, Son, and Holy Ghost.

"All Praise to Thee, My God, This Night"
by Thomas Ken, 1709
(author's adaptation)

Refrain:
May this night be one of peace and may my bed be one of rest.
Fill my dreams with thoughts of you
And wake me ready for another day.

The Lord's Prayer:
Our Father, who art in heaven,
Hallowed be thy name.
Thy kingdom come,
Thy will be done on earth,
As it is in heaven.
Give us this day our daily bread.
And forgive us our sins, as we forgive those who sin against us.
And lead us not into temptation, but deliver us from evil.
For thine is the kingdom, and the power, and the glory,
forever and ever.

Today's Prayer:

Everything I have ever seen, everything I have ever read, every inch of creation that ever existed was created by you. All of it is yours. From the sunrise to the greatest mountains to the plankton in the seas, it is all yours. I sit surrounded by your creation, knowing that just like the sand and the sea, I am created by you. I am yours. Today, help me to remember that. Help me rest in the knowledge that I have been created by a loving God.

Concluding Prayer:

I will lay down in my bed knowing that there are those who will not sleep peacefully this night. Be with those who suffer and grieve tonight. Be with those who cry themselves to sleep. Bring my day to a peaceful end and give me the centered feeling that only your presence can provide as I close my eyes and rest in you. *Amen.*

MIDNIGHT PRAYER

Call to Prayer:
Day or night your presence persists.
    Your glory has no end.

Invitation:
The heavens proclaim the glory of God.
    The skies display his craftsmanship.
Day after day they continue to speak;
    night after night they make him known.
They speak without a sound or word;
    their voice is never heard.
Yet their message has gone throughout the earth,
    and their words to all the world.

Psalm 19:1-4a

Refrain:
Indeed, he who watches over Israel never slumbers or sleeps.

Psalm 121:4

Reading:
This is all the more urgent, for you know how late it is; time is running out. Wake up, for our salvation is nearer now than when we first believed. The night is almost gone; the day of salvation will soon be here. So remove your dark deeds like dirty clothes, and put on the shining armor of right living. Because we belong to the day, we must live decent lives for all to see. Don't participate in the darkness of wild parties and drunkenness, or in sexual promiscuity and immoral living, or in quarreling and jealousy. Instead, clothe yourself with the presence of the Lord Jesus Christ. And don't let yourself think about ways to indulge your evil desires.

Romans 13:11-14

Refrain:
Indeed, he who watches over Israel never slumbers or sleeps.

Psalm 121:4

Psalm:
I, I am the man that has known
    Distress by the stroke of his rod,
And still through the pain I groan
    And long for the absence of God.
The happy in Jesus may sleep,
    But, in me he still appears.
It is now my time to weep
    And water my couch with my tears.

Or rather, if any are close,
    Sad and afflicted like me,
All night let us lift up our cry
    And mourn his appearing to see,
As watchmen expecting the morn.
    Look out for the light of his face
And wait for his mercy's return
    And long to recover his grace.

His grace to our souls did appear
    And brought us salvation from sin.
We felt our Immanuel here,
    Restoring his kingdom within.
And yet we have lost him again.
    His Spirit has taken its flight.
Our joy is turned into pain;
    Our day it is turned into night.

O, what shall we do to retrieve
    The love we had for a season.
It is better to die than to live
    Exiled from the presence of God,
With sorrow distracted and doubt.
    With palpable horror, oppressed,
The city we wander about
    And seek our rest on his chest.

You watchmen of Israel declare
    If you our Beloved have seen,
And point to that Heavenly Fair,
    Surpassing the children of men.
Our Lover and Lord from above,
    Who alone can quiet our pain,
Who only we languish to love—
    O, where shall we find him again?

The joy and desire of our eyes,
    The end of our sorrow and woe.
Our hope and our heavenly prize,
    Our height of ambition below.
Once more if he show us his face,
    He never again shall depart.
Detained in our closest embrace,
    Eternally held in our heart.

"I, I Am the Man That Hath Known"
by Charles Wesley, 1740
(author's adaptation)

Refrain:
Indeed, he who watches over Israel never slumbers or sleeps.

Psalm 121:4

The Lord's Prayer:
Our Father, who art in heaven,
Hallowed be thy name.
Thy kingdom come,
Thy will be done on earth,
As it is in heaven.
Give us this day our daily bread.
And forgive us our sins, as we forgive those who sin against us.
And lead us not into temptation, but deliver us from evil.
For thine is the kingdom, and the power, and the glory,
forever and ever.

Today's Prayer:
Everything I have ever seen, everything I have ever read, every inch of creation that ever existed was created by you. All of it is yours. From the sunrise to the greatest mountains to the plankton in the seas, it is all yours. I sit surrounded by your creation, knowing that just like the sand and the sea, I am created by you. I am yours. Today, help me to remember that. Help me rest in the knowledge that I have been created by a loving God.

Concluding Prayer:
Guide me waking and guard me sleeping that awake I may watch with you and asleep I may rest in peace. *Amen.*

from *The Book of Common Prayer*

FRIDAY

DAWN PRAYER

Call to Prayer:
Praise God in his sanctuary;
   praise him in his mighty heaven!
Praise him for his mighty works;
   praise his unequaled greatness!
Praise him with a blast of the ram's horn;
   praise him with the lyre and harp!
Praise him with the tambourine and dancing;
   praise him with strings and flutes!
Praise him with a clash of cymbals;
   praise him with loud clanging cymbals.
Let everything that breathes sing praises to the LORD!
   Praise the LORD!

Psalm 150

Invitation:
As the dawn brings dew for the morning, I bring praise for your name.
   I bring a readiness to hear;
   I bring a spirit of prayer.

Refrain:
Then your salvation will come like the dawn,
      and your wounds will quickly heal.
   Your godliness will lead you forward,
      and the glory of the LORD will protect you from behind.

Isaiah 58:8

Reading:
Sell your possessions and give to those in need. This will store up treasure for you in heaven! And the purses of heaven never get old or develop holes. Your treasure will be safe; no thief can steal it and no moth can destroy it. Wherever your treasure is, there the desires of your heart will also be.

   Be dressed for service and keep your lamps burning, as though you were waiting for your master to return from the wedding feast. Then you will be ready to open the door and let him in the moment he arrives and knocks. The servants who are ready and waiting for his return will be rewarded. I tell you the truth, he himself will seat them, put on an apron, and serve them as they sit and eat! He may come in the middle of the night or just before dawn. But whenever he comes, he will reward the servants who are ready.

Understand this: If a homeowner knew exactly when a burglar was coming, he would not permit his house to be broken into. You also must be ready all the time, for the Son of Man will come when least expected.

Luke 12:22-40

Refrain:

Then your salvation will come like the dawn,
and your wounds will quickly heal.
Your godliness will lead you forward,
and the glory of the LORD will protect you from behind.

Isaiah 58:8

Psalm:

Honor the LORD, you heavenly beings;
honor the LORD for his glory and strength.
Honor the LORD for the glory of his name.
Worship the LORD in the splendor of his holiness.
The voice of the LORD echoes above the sea.
The God of glory thunders.
The LORD thunders over the mighty sea.
The voice of the LORD is powerful;
the voice of the LORD is majestic.
The voice of the LORD splits the mighty cedars;
the LORD shatters the cedars of Lebanon.
He makes Lebanon's mountains skip like a calf;
he makes Mount Hermon leap like a young wild ox.
The voice of the LORD strikes
with bolts of lightning.
The voice of the LORD makes the barren wilderness quake;

the LORD shakes the wilderness of Kadesh.
The voice of the LORD twists mighty oaks
    and strips the forests bare.
The LORD rules over the floodwaters.
    The LORD reigns as king forever.
The LORD gives his people strength.
    The LORD blesses them with peace.

Psalm 29

Refrain:
Then your salvation will come like the dawn,
    and your wounds will quickly heal.
  Your godliness will lead you forward,
    and the glory of the LORD will protect you from behind.

Isaiah 58:8

The Lord's Prayer:
Our Father, who art in heaven,
Hallowed be thy name.
Thy kingdom come,
Thy will be done on earth,
As it is in heaven.
Give us this day our daily bread.
And forgive us our sins, as we forgive those who sin against us.
And lead us not into temptation, but deliver us from evil.
For thine is the kingdom, and the power, and the glory,
forever and ever.

Today's Prayer:
You loved me before I knew what love was. You began blessing me
before I drew my first breath. You have never left me alone. Even in
the darkest times, even in the saddest times, you were there. Surely
your goodness has known no bounds in my life. As this week draws
to a close, heal the places where I've been wounded this week, protect
me as I go, and give me the grace to see your goodness in every place,
in every moment. Show me your presence that moves me forward in
the glory of your name.

Concluding Prayer:

The earliest rays of the sun fill the skies with magic and plant the seeds of possibility in my soul. Let this sprout of excitement fill this new day with growth. Wherever I go, and whatever becomes today's story, help me approach it with the feeling of the dawn. Help me to capture the potential of every moment and see every breath I breathe and every step I take to make your kingdom break forth like the dawn of a new day in the world. *Amen.*

MORNING PRAYER

Call to Prayer:
Great is his faithfulness;
> his mercies begin afresh each morning.

Lamentations 3:23

Confession:
God of grace and mercy, hear my cries.
> I have sinned against you.

I have done things that I am ashamed of;
> I have done things that I should be ashamed of but I'm not;
> And I have ignored things that I should have acted on.

Will you forgive my actions and inaction?
Will you give me undeserved grace and mercy again?
Will you push me forward in the opposite direction of sin,
> So that I might serve you with all I am
> And bring glory to your name?

Invitation:
It is good to proclaim your unfailing love in the morning,
> your faithfulness in the evening…

Psalm 92:2

Refrain:
But as for me, I will sing about your power.
> Each morning I will sing with joy about your unfailing love.
> For you have been my refuge,
> a place of safety when I am in distress.

Psalm 59:16

Reading:
So humble yourselves before God. Resist the devil, and he will flee from you. Come close to God, and God will come close to you. Wash your hands, you sinners; purify your hearts, for your loyalty is divided between God and the world. Let there by tears for what you have done. Let there be sorrow and deep grief. Let there be sadness

instead of laughter, and gloom instead of joy. Humble yourselves before the Lord, and he will lift you up in honor.

Don't speak evil against each other, dear brothers and sisters. If you criticize and judge each other, then you are criticizing and judging God's law. But your job is to obey the law, not to judge whether it applies to you. God alone, who gave the law, is the Judge. He alone has the power to save or to destroy. So what right do you have to judge your neighbor?

Look here, you who say, "Today or tomorrow we are going to a certain town and will stay there a year. We will do business there and make a profit. How do you know what your life will be like tomorrow? Your life is like the morning fog—it's here a little while, then it's gone. What you ought to say is, "If the Lord wants us to, we will live and do this or that." Otherwise you are boasting about your own pretentious plans, and all such boasting is evil.

James 4:7-16

Refrain:

But as for me, I will sing about your power.
> Each morning I will sing with joy about your unfailing love.
For you have been my refuge,
> a place of safety when I am in distress.

Psalm 59:16

Psalm:

Every morning the red sun
Rises warm and bright;
But the evening comes on,
And the cold, dark night.
There's a bright land far away
Where it is never-ending day.

Every spring the sweet young flowers
Open fresh and glad,
Till the chilly autumn hours
Wither them away!
There's a land we have not seen,
Where the trees are always green.

Little birds sing songs of praise
All the summer long.
But in colder, shorter days
They forget their song.
There's a place where angels sing
Ceaseless praises to their King.

Christ our Lord is ever near
Those who follow him!
But we cannot see him here,
For our eyes are dim.
There is a most happy place,
Where we'll always see his face.

Who shall go to that fair land?
All who love the right.
Holy children there shall stand,
In their robes of white.
In that heaven so bright and blest,
Is our everlasting rest.

"Every Morning the Red Sun"
by Cecil Frances Alexander, 1848
(author's adaptation)

Refrain:
But as for me, I will sing about your power.
Each morning I will sing with joy about your unfailing love.
For you have been my refuge,
a place of safety when I am in distress.

Psalm 59:16

The Lord's Prayer:
Our Father, who art in heaven,
Hallowed be thy name.
Thy kingdom come,
Thy will be done on earth,
As it is in heaven.
Give us this day our daily bread.

And forgive us our sins, as we forgive those who sin against us.
And lead us not into temptation, but deliver us from evil.
For thine is the kingdom, and the power, and the glory,
forever and ever.

Today's Prayer:

You loved me before I knew what love was. You began blessing me
before I drew my first breath. You have never left me alone. Even in
the darkest times, even in the saddest times, you were there. Surely
your goodness has known no bounds in my life. As this week draws
to a close, heal the places where I've been wounded this week, protect
me as I go, and give me the grace to see your goodness in every place,
in every moment. Show me your presence that moves me forward in
the glory of your name.

Concluding Prayer:

Your love never ends. Your love never fails. Like the faithfulness of
the rotation of the earth, bringing morning after morning, your love
never ends. It holds me close, pushes me forward, and becomes a safe
shelter in times of trouble. This day let me see your love as it calls me
beyond myself and as it comforts me when I am unsure. Then, when
things get difficult, guide me to the refuge of your loving arms and let
me hide myself in you as I face all of what this day will throw at me.
Amen.

NOONDAY PRAYER

Call to Prayer:
Your love is as faithful as the noonday sun
    Bringing life to my soul,
    Bringing life to my soul.

Invitation:
Be still in the presence of the LORD,
    and wait patiently for him to act.

Psalm 37:7a

Refrain:
Show me the right path, O LORD;
    point out the road for me to follow.
Lead me by your truth and teach me,
    for you are the God who saves me.
All day long I put my hope in you.

Psalm 25:4-5

Psalm:
At the gate that leads to glory, from the rugged path of sin,
Where the joys that fill the soul are ever new,
O ye weary, heavy-laden, will you strive to enter in,
While the Savior now is waiting there for you?

Strait is the gate and narrow is the way
That leads to life above;
Strive to enter in, oh, strive to enter in!
Come to a Savior's love.

At the gate that leads to glory there's a light that shines still.
It is the pure and holy light of promise true.
Hear the blessed invitation to whosoever will,
From the Savior who is waiting now for you.

Strait is the gate and narrow is the way
That leads to life above;
Strive to enter in, oh, strive to enter in!
Come to a Savior's love.

At the gate that leads to glory you will never knock in vain.
There is room for everyone, and welcome too.
Only give your heart to Jesus, life eternal you will gain.
He is calling, he is waiting now for you.

Strait is the gate and narrow is the way
That leads to life above;
Strive to enter in, oh, strive to enter in!
Come to a Savior's love.

From the gate that leads to glory, oh, how many go astray!
We are told that they that find it are but few.
Then believe the words of Jesus, enter quickly while you may.
He is waiting now with open arms for you.

Strait is the gate and narrow is the way
That leads to life above;
Strive to enter in, oh, strive to enter in!
Come to a Savior's love.

"Strait Is the Gate and Narrow Is the Way"
by Henrietta E. Blair (aka, Fanny Crosby), 1885
(author's adaptation)

Refrain:
Show me the right path, O LORD;
    point out the road for me to follow.
Lead me by your truth and teach me,
    for you are the God who saves me.
All day long I put my hope in you.

Psalm 25:4-5

The Lord's Prayer:
Our Father, who art in heaven,
Hallowed be thy name.
Thy kingdom come,
Thy will be done on earth,
As it is in heaven.
Give us this day our daily bread.
And forgive us our sins, as we forgive those who sin against us.
And lead us not into temptation, but deliver us from evil.
For thine is the kingdom, and the power, and the glory,
forever and ever.

Today's Prayer:
You loved me before I knew what love was. You began blessing me before I drew my first breath. You have never left me alone. Even in the darkest times, even in the saddest times, you were there. Surely your goodness has known no bounds in my life. As this week draws to a close, heal the places where I've been wounded this week, protect me as I go and give me the grace to see your goodness in every place, in every moment. Show me your presence that moves me forward in the glory of your name.

Concluding Prayer:
Creator, Savior, Friend, you have walked with me all day today. Now, at the middle of the day, show me where I have lost my way. Show me where I took steps off the path that I began to try and follow in the beginning of this day. I want to be on the right path: the one you have for me. God, lead me, guide me that I might walk on the narrow path that leads to life and bring glory to your name. *Amen.*

AFTERNOON/AFTER SCHOOL PRAYER

Call to Prayer:
Truly God is good to Israel,
    to those whose hearts are pure.

Psalm 73:1

Confession
O LORD, I have come to you for protection;
    don't let me be disgraced.
Save me, for you do what is right.
Turn your ear to listen to me;
    rescue me quickly.
Be my rock of protection,
    a fortress where I will be safe.

Psalm 31:1-2

Invitation:
Here I am. The real me.
    The broken me.
    The needy me.
    The me with doubts.
Bring your presence in the middle of my mess,
    In the middle of my doubts
    In the middle of my needs
    In the middle of my brokenness.
Fill all of that with all of you, and let me see past myself
    Into your heart.

Refrain:
I will praise you, LORD, with all my heart;
    I will tell of all the marvelous things you have done.

Psalm 9:1

Reading:

That Sunday evening the disciples were meeting behind locked doors because they were afraid of the Jewish leaders. Suddenly, Jesus was standing there among them! "Peace be with you," he said. As he spoke, he showed them the wounds in his hands and his side. They were filled with joy when they saw the Lord! Again he said, "Peace be with you. As the Father has sent me, so I am sending you." Then he breathed on them and said, "Receive the Holy Spirit. If you forgive anyone's sins, they are forgiven. If you do not forgive them, they are not forgiven."

One of the twelve disciples, Thomas (nicknamed the Twin), was not with the others when Jesus came. They told him, "We have seen the Lord!" But he replied, "I won't believe it unless I see the nail wounds in his hands, put my fingers into them, and place my hand into the wound in his side."

Eight days later the disciples were together again, and this time Thomas was with them. The doors were locked; but suddenly, as before, Jesus was standing among them. "Peace be with you," he said. Then he said to Thomas, "Put your finger here, and look at my hands. Put your hand into the wound in my side. Don't be faithless any longer. Believe!"

"My Lord and my God!" Thomas exclaimed.

Then Jesus told him, "You believe because you have seen me. Blessed are those who believe without seeing me."

John 20:19-29

Refrain:

I will praise you, LORD, with all my heart;
   I will tell of all the marvelous things you have done.

Psalm 9:1

Psalm:

All the way my Savior leads me;
What have I to ask beside?
Can I doubt his tender mercy,
Who through life has been my Guide?
Heavenly peace, divine comfort,
Here by faith in him to dwell!

For I know, whatever happens to me,
Jesus does all things well;
For I know, whatever happens to me,
Jesus does all things well.

All the way my Savior leads me,
Cheers each winding path I tread;
Gives me grace for every trial,
Feeds me with the living Bread.
Though my weary steps may falter,
And my soul thirsty may be,
Gushing from the Rock before me,
Behold! A spring of joy I see;
Gushing from the Rock before me,
Behold! A spring of joy I see.

All the way my Savior leads me
O the fullness of his love!
Perfect rest to me is promised
In my Father's house above.
When my spirit, mortally clothed,
Wings its flight to realms of day
This my song through endless ages—
Jesus led me all the way;
This my song through endless ages—
Jesus led me all the way.

"All the Way My Savior Leads Me"
by Fanny Crosby, 1875
(author's adaptation)

Refrain:

I will praise you, LORD, with all my heart;
I will tell of all the marvelous things you have done.

Psalm 9:1

The Lord's Prayer:

Our Father, who art in heaven,
Hallowed be thy name.
Thy kingdom come,
Thy will be done on earth,
As it is in heaven.
Give us this day our daily bread.
And forgive us our sins, as we forgive those who sin against us.
And lead us not into temptation, but deliver us from evil.
For thine is the kingdom, and the power, and the glory,
forever and ever.

Today's Prayer:

You loved me before I knew what love was. You began blessing me
before I drew my first breath. You have never left me alone. Even in
the darkest times, even in the saddest times, you were there. Surely
your goodness has known no bounds in my life. As this week draws
to a close, heal the places where I've been wounded this week, protect
me as I go, and give me the grace to see your goodness in every place,
in every moment. Show me your presence that moves me forward in
the glory of your name.

Concluding Prayer:

You know my questions. You know my doubts. You know all the
secret things that hide deep within my heart, yet you love me. I
don't understand how that is possible, but I give you thanks for your
unfathomable love. I pray that as I move through the end of this
day you will reveal yourself to me like you did to Thomas and the
disciples. Show me the things I need to see. Tell me the things I need
to hear that I might stay close to you through the final hours of this
day. *Amen.*

END OF DAY PRAYER

Call to Prayer:
May the Lord Almighty grant me and those I love a peaceful night
and a perfect end.

from The Book of Common Prayer

Confession:
Almighty Savior, I confess that I have sinned today.

Search my heart and reveal to me my sins, that I may turn from
them and follow you.

> *Go hour by hour, reflecting on your day and where you have
> sinned.*
> *Face up to your sin, asking for forgiveness, and then ask God how
> you can improve tomorrow.*

Invitation:
You are right here among us, LORD.
We are known as your people.
Please don't abandon us now!

Jeremiah 14:9b

Refrain:
O LORD God of Heaven's Armies, hear my prayer.
Listen, O God of Jacob.

Psalm 84:8

Reading:
Since you have been raised to new life with Christ, set your sights
on the realities of heaven, where Christ sits in the place of honor at
God's right hand. Think about the things of heaven, not the things of
earth. For you died to this life, and your real life is hidden with Christ
in God. And when Christ, who is your life, is revealed to the whole
world, you will share in all his glory.

So put to death the sinful, earthly things lurking within you.
Have nothing to do with sexual immorality, impurity, lust, and evil

desires. Don't be greedy, for a greedy person is an idolater, worshiping the things of this world. Because of these sins, the anger of God is coming. You used to do these things when your life was still part of this world. But now is the time to get rid of anger, rage, malicious behavior, slander, and dirty language. Don't lie to each other, for you have stripped off your old sinful nature and all its wicked deeds. Put on your new nature, and be renewed as you learn to know your Creator and become like him. In this new life, it doesn't matter if you are a Jew or a Gentile, circumcised or uncircumcised, barbaric, uncivilized, slave, or free. Christ is all that matters, and he lives in all of us.

Since God chose you to be the holy people he loves, you must clothe yourselves with tenderhearted mercy, kindness, humility, gentleness, and patience. Make allowance for each other's faults, and forgive anyone who offends you. Remember, the Lord forgave you, so you must forgive others. Above all, clothe yourselves with love, which binds us all together in perfect harmony. And let the peace that comes from Christ rule in your hearts. For as members of one body you are called to live in peace. And always be thankful.

Let the message about Christ, in all its richness, fill your lives. Teach and counsel each other with all the wisdom he gives. Sing psalms and hymns and spiritual songs to God with thankful hearts. And whatever you do or say, do it as a representative of the Lord Jesus, giving thanks through him to God the Father.

Colossians 3:1-17

Refrain:

O LORD God of Heaven's Armies, hear my prayer.
Listen, O God of Jacob.

Psalm 84:8

Psalm:

I waited patiently for the LORD to help me,
and he turned to me and heard my cry.
He lifted me out of the pit of despair,
out of the mud and the mire.
He set my feet on solid ground
and steadied me as I walked along.

He has given me a new song to sing,
    a hymn of praise to our God.
Many will see what he has done and be amazed.
    They will put their trust in the LORD.
Oh, the joys of those who trust the LORD,
    who have no confidence in the proud
    or in those who worship idols.
O LORD my God, you have performed many wonders for us.
    Your plans for us are too numerous to list.
    You have no equal.
If I tried to recite all your wonderful deeds,
    I would never come to the end of them.
You take no delight in sacrifices or offerings.
    Now that you have made me listen, I finally understand—
    you don't require burnt offerings or sin offerings.
Then I said, "Look, I have come.
    As is written about me in the Scriptures:
I take joy in doing your will, my God,
    for your instructions are written on my heart."
I have told all your people about your justice.
    I have not been afraid to speak out,
    as you, O LORD, well know.
I have not kept the good news of your justice hidden in my heart;
    I have talked about your faithfulness and saving power.
I have told everyone in the great assembly
    of your unfailing love and faithfulness.
LORD, don't hold back your tender mercies from me.
    Let your unfailing love and faithfulness always protect me.
For troubles surround me—
    too many to count!
My sins pile up so high
    I can't see my way out.
They outnumber the hairs on my head.
    I have lost all courage.
Please, LORD, rescue me!
    Come quickly, LORD, and help me.
May those who try to destroy me
    be humiliated and put to shame.

May those who take delight in my trouble
    be turned back in disgrace.
Let them be horrified by their shame,
    for they said, "Aha! We've got him now!"
But may all who search for you
    be filled with joy and gladness in you.
May those who love your salvation
    repeatedly shout, "The LORD is great!"
As for me, since I am poor and needy,
    let the LORD keep me in his thoughts.
You are my helper and my savior.
    O my God, do not delay.

Psalm 40

Refrain:

O LORD God of Heaven's Armies, hear my prayer.
    Listen, O God of Jacob.

Psalm 84:8

The Lord's Prayer:

Our Father, who art in heaven,
Hallowed be thy name.
Thy kingdom come,
Thy will be done on earth,
As it is in heaven.
Give us this day our daily bread.
And forgive us our sins, as we forgive those who sin against us.
And lead us not into temptation, but deliver us from evil.
For thine is the kingdom, and the power, and the glory,
forever and ever.

Today's Prayer:

You loved me before I knew what love was. You began blessing me before I drew my first breath. You have never left me alone. Even in the darkest times, even in the saddest times, you were there. Surely your goodness has known no bounds in my life. As this week draws to a close, heal the places where I've been wounded this week, protect me as I go, and give me the grace to see your goodness in every place, in every moment. Show me your presence that moves me forward in the glory of your name.

Concluding Prayer:
Be my light in the darkness, O Lord, and in your great mercy defend me from all dangers of this night, for the love of your only Son, my Savior Jesus Christ. *Amen.*

MIDNIGHT PRAYER

Call to Prayer:
I rise at midnight to thank you
    for your just regulations.

Psalm 119:62

Invitation:
At midnight they were roused by the shout, "Look, the bridegroom is coming! Come out and meet him!"

Matthew 25:6

Refrain:
The LORD gives his people strength.
    The LORD blesses them with peace.

Psalm 29:11

Reading:
Then Jesus went with them to the olive grove called Gethsemane, and he said, "Sit here while I go over there to pray." He took Peter and Zebedee's two sons, James and John, and he became anguished and distressed. He told them, "My soul is crushed with grief to the point of death. Stay here and keep watch with me."

He went on a little farther and bowed with his face to the ground, praying, "My Father! If it is possible, let this cup of suffering be taken away from me. Yet I want your will to be done, not mine."

Then he returned to the disciples and found them asleep. He said to Peter, "Couldn't you watch with me even one hour? Keep watch and pray, so that you will not give in to temptation. For the spirit is willing, but the body is weak!"

Then Jesus left them a second time and prayed, "My Father! If this cup cannot be taken away unless I drink it, your will be done." When he returned to them again, he found them sleeping, for they couldn't keep their eyes open.

So he went to pray a third time, saying the same things again. Then he came to the disciples and said, "Go ahead and sleep. Have your rest. But look—the time has come. The Son of Man is betrayed into the hands of sinners. Up, let's be going. Look, my betrayer is here!"

Matthew 26:36-46

Refrain:
The LORD gives his people strength.
The LORD blesses them with peace.

Psalm 29:11

Psalm:
"Wake, awake, for night is flying,"
the watchmen on the heights are crying;
"Awake, Jerusalem, arise!"
Midnight hears the welcome voices
and at the thrilling cry rejoices:
"Where are the virgins pure and wise?
The Bridegroom comes: Awake!
Your lamps with gladness take!
Alleluia! With bridal care and faith's bold prayer,
to meet the Bridegroom, come, prepare!"

Zion hears the watchmen singing,
and in her heart new joy is springing.
She wakes, she rises from her gloom.
For her Lord comes down all-glorious
and strong in grace, in truth victorious.
Her star is risen, her light is come!
Now come, O Blessed One,
Lord Jesus, God's own Son.
Sing hosanna!
We answer all in joy your call;
we follow to the wedding hall.

Lamb of God, the heavens adore you,
the saints and angels sing before you
with harp and cymbals' clearest tone.
Of one pearl each shining portal,
where, joining with the choir immortal,

we gather round your radiant throne.
No eye has seen that light,
no ear the echoed might of your glory;
yet there shall we in victory
sing shouts of joy eternally!

"Wake, Awake, for Night Is Flying"
by Catherine Winkworth and Philipp Nicolai, 1599
(author's adaptation)

Refrain:

The LORD gives his people strength.
The LORD blesses them with peace.

Psalm 29:11

The Lord's Prayer:

Our Father, who art in heaven,
Hallowed be thy name.
Thy kingdom come,
Thy will be done on earth,
As it is in heaven.
Give us this day our daily bread.
And forgive us our sins, as we forgive those who sin against us.
And lead us not into temptation, but deliver us from evil.
For thine is the kingdom, and the power, and the glory,
forever and ever.

Today's Prayer:

You loved me before I knew what love was. You began blessing me
before I drew my first breath. You have never left me alone. Even in
the darkest times, even in the saddest times, you were there. Surely
your goodness has known no bounds in my life. As this week draws
to a close, heal the places where I've been wounded this week, protect
me as I go, and give me the grace to see your goodness in every place,
in every moment. Show me your presence that moves me forward in
the glory of your name.

Concluding Prayer:
May the Lord bless us and keep us and make his face to shine upon us from this day forth and forever more. *Amen.*

SATURDAY

DAWN PRAYER

Call to Prayer:

The way of the righteous is like the first gleam of dawn,
>   which shines ever brighter until the full light of day.

Proverbs 4:18

Invitation:

Wake up, my heart!
>   Wake up, O lyre and harp!
>   I will wake the dawn with my song.

I will thank you, Lord, among all the people.
>   I will sing your praises among the nations.

Psalm 57:8-9

Refrain:

Holy Spirit, rise up in my heart like the sun on the horizon at dawn.
>   Break forth through the darkness in my heart
>   And fill me with your light.

Reading:

Therefore, I will always remind you about these things—even though you already know them and are standing firm in the truth you have been taught. And it is only right that I should keep on reminding you as long as I live. For our Lord Jesus Christ has shown me that I must soon leave this earthly life, so I will work hard to make sure you always remember these things after I am gone.

For we were not making up clever stories when we told you about the powerful coming of our Lord Jesus Christ. We saw his majestic splendor with our own eyes when he received honor and glory from God the Father. The voice from the majestic glory of God said to him, "This is my dearly loved Son, who brings me great joy." We ourselves heard that voice from heaven when we were with him on the holy mountain.

Because of that experience, we have even greater confidence in the message proclaimed by the prophets. You must pay close attention to what they wrote, for their words are like a lamp shining in a dark place—until the Day dawns, and Christ the Morning Star shines in your hearts. Above all, you must realize that no prophecy in Scripture ever came from the prophet's own understanding, or from human initiative. No, those prophets were moved by the Holy Spirit, and they spoke from God.

2 Peter 1:12-21

Refrain:
Holy Spirit, rise up in my heart like the sun on the horizon at dawn.
>Break forth through the darkness in my heart
>And fill me with your light.

Psalm:
LORD, our Lord,
>how majestic is your name in all the earth!
You have set your glory
>in the heavens.
Through the praise of children and infants
>you have established a stronghold against your enemies,
>to silence the foe and the avenger.
When I consider your heavens,
>the work of your fingers,
the moon and the stars,
>which you have set in place,
what is mankind that you are mindful of them,
>human beings that you care for them?
You have made them a little lower than the angels
>and crowned them with glory and honor.
You made them rulers over the works of your hands;
>you put everything under their feet:
all flocks and herds,
>and the animals of the wild,
the birds in the sky,
>and the fish in the sea,
>all that swim the paths of the seas.
LORD, our Lord,
>how majestic is your name in all the earth!

Psalm 8 (NIV)

Refrain:
Holy Spirit, rise up in my heart like the sun on the horizon at dawn.
    Break forth through the darkness in my heart
    And fill me with your light.

The Lord's Prayer:
Our Father, who art in heaven,
Hallowed be thy name.
Thy kingdom come,
Thy will be done on earth,
As it is in heaven.
Give us this day our daily bread.
And forgive us our sins, as we forgive those who sin against us.
And lead us not into temptation, but deliver us from evil.
For thine is the kingdom, and the power, and the glory,
forever and ever.

Today's Prayer:
I thank you that you do not require us to be serious all the time.
Thank you that you do not call us to a life of unending work. I thank
you for the gift of fun, the gift of laughter, the gift of recreation. Help
me to learn to follow your Spirit into the moments when I can let go
of the list of things to be done and rest, relax, and play. Show me how
to be aware of your presence in those times today. Fill my fun with
your Spirit.

Concluding Prayer:
Like the morning flowers that open at the first touch of sunlight, may
the most beautiful, enjoyable parts of my life open wide to me today.
May it be a day full of happiness, pleasure, and joy. Though I know
there will be things that need to be done, fill them with the power of
fun, so I might sing your praises through the rest and work ahead of
me this day. *Amen.*

MORNING PRAYER

Call to Prayer:
If I ride the wings of the morning,
    if I dwell by the farthest oceans,
even there your hand will guide me,
    and your strength will support me.

Psalm 139:9-10

Confession:
Even at the beginning of my day I find myself in need of your
forgiveness.
    For my thoughts
    For my words
    For my actions

I ask for your forgiveness, and your protection.
Protect me form all the distractions that line the path ahead of me
today.
Protect me from my own temptations that threaten to overtake my
desire for holiness.

May today be a day that I work out my salvation, empowered by our
Holy Spirit.

Invitation:
You are worthy of my praise in the morning.
    Call forth from my heart a soul-deep thankfulness
    That I may not be able to stop singing your praise.

Refrain:
Be merciful to me, O Lord,
    for I am calling on you constantly.
Give me happiness, O Lord,
    for I give myself to you.

Psalm 86:3-4

Reading:

So at last the king gave orders for Daniel to be arrested and thrown into the den of lions. The king said to him, "May your God, whom you serve so faithfully, rescue you."

A stone was brought and placed over the mouth of the den. The king sealed the stone with his own royal seal and the seals of his nobles, so that no one could rescue Daniel. Then the king returned to his palace and spent the night fasting. He refused his usual entertainment and couldn't sleep at all that night.

Very early the next morning, the king got up and hurried out to the lions' den. When he got there, he called out in anguish, "Daniel, servant of the living God! Was your God, whom you serve so faithfully, able to rescue you from the lions?"

Daniel answered, "Long live the king! My God sent his angel to shut the lions' mouths so that they would not hurt me, for I have been found innocent in his sight. And I have not wronged you, Your Majesty."

The king was overjoyed and ordered that Daniel be lifted from the den. Not a scratch was found on him, for he had trusted in his God.

Then the king gave orders to arrest the men who had maliciously accused Daniel. He had them thrown into the lions' den, along with their wives and children. The lions leaped on them and tore them apart before they even hit the floor of the den.

Then King Darius sent this message to the people of every race and nation and language throughout the world:

"Peace and prosperity to you! I decree that everyone throughout my kingdom should tremble with fear before the God of Daniel.

For he is the living God,
    and he will endure forever.
His kingdom will never be destroyed,
    and his rule will never end.
He rescues and saves his people;
He performs miraculous signs and wonders
    in the heavens and on earth.
He has rescued Daniel
    from the power of the lions."

Daniel 6:16-27

Refrain:

Be merciful to me, O Lord,
for I am calling on you constantly.
Give me happiness, O Lord,
for I give myself to you.

Psalm 86:3-4

Psalm:

All hail, blessed morning,
With sunshine adorning
The world that lay weeping over him that was slain.
You come with gladness,
Dispelling our sadness,
You bring good tidings: he lives again.

Our Rock is secure,
Our Anchor is sure.
The Lord our Redeemer is mighty to save.
Go, heralds of glory,
And publish the story
That Jesus has triumphed over death and the grave.

No more shall he languish
Or suffer the anguish
He bore on the cross when his blood was shed.
Behold! Angels in wonder,
The grave torn asunder,
Beheld when their Monarch arose from the dead.

Our Rock is secure,
Our Anchor is sure.
The Lord our Redeemer is mighty to save.
Go, heralds of glory,
And publish the story
That Jesus has triumphed over death and the grave.

He lives victorious,
He lives all-glorious.

THE BOOK OF EVERYDAY PRAYER

Through him shall the captive from bondage be free.
The volume of ages
Proclaims on its pages,
Forever established his kingdom will be.

Our Rock is secure,
Our Anchor is sure.
The Lord our Redeemer is mighty to save.
Go, heralds of glory,
And publish the story
That Jesus has triumphed over death and the grave.

Then, while we adore him,
And gather before him,
Our hearts and our voices united shall praise
The great Intercessor
For every transgressor,
The Son of the Highest, the Ancient of days.

"All Hail, Blessed Morning"
by Fanny Crosby, 1883
(author's adaptation)

Refrain:
Be merciful to me, O Lord,
    for I am calling on you constantly.
Give me happiness, O Lord,
    for I give myself to you.

Psalm 86:3-4

The Lord's Prayer:
Our Father, who art in heaven,
Hallowed be thy name.
Thy kingdom come,
Thy will be done on earth,
As it is in heaven.
Give us this day our daily bread.
And forgive us our sins, as we forgive those who sin against us.
And lead us not into temptation, but deliver us from evil.

For thine is the kingdom, and the power, and the glory,
forever and ever.

Today's Prayer:

I thank you that you do not require us to be serious all the time.
Thank you that you do not call us to a life of unending work. I thank
you for the gift of fun, the gift of laughter, the gift of recreation. Help
me to learn to follow your Spirit into the moments when I can let go
of the list of things to be done and rest, relax, and play. Show me how
to be aware of your presence in those times today. Fill my fun with
your Spirit.

Concluding Prayer:

This morning, the beginning of this day, holds in it a world of
possibilities. Will you give me the courage to take hold of those
possibilities this day? May I not squander its potential. May I not miss
the wonderful opportunities for prayer, ministry, relaxation, and fun.
May I take hold of this day and live it to fullness. Empower me by
your Spirit to use this day to draw me and those around me closer to
you. *Amen.*

NOONDAY PRAYER

Call to Prayer:
Praise God who causes the sun to rise on the righteous and
unrighteous,
> Giving light and life to all the children of the earth,
> Nourishing the lilies of the field and the wheat on the plain.

Invitation:
Your grace is as boundless as the skies,
> Your faithfulness like the tides.
You are truly worthy of my praise.
> My heart longs for your presence.

Refrain:
Feed the hungry,
> and help those in trouble.
Then your light will shine out from the darkness,
> and the darkness around you will be as bright as noon.

Isaiah 58:10

Psalm:
Here I may be weak and poor,
With afflictions to endure;
All about me not a ray of light to see.
Just as he has often done,
For his helpless trusting ones,
God has promised to provide for me.

God has promised to provide for me,
God has promised to provide for me.
All creation is his own,
All my needs to him are known.
He has promised to provide for me.

All my clothing and my food,
And my health and all that's good

Are within his own written guarantee.
God is caring for the poor,
Just as he has done before.
He has promised to provide for me.

Mighty men may have control
Of the silver and the gold.
Want and sorrow for the poor there may be,
But the God of heaven reigns,
And his promise is the same,
And I know he will provide for me.

Ancient Israel heard his voice.
How the people did rejoice,
When he led them safely through the mighty sea.
In the wilderness they knew,
What the living God can do,
He's the one that doth provide for me.

When they hadn't any bread,
Good old Moses knelt and pray'd;
And the God who gives so plentiful and free,
Sent the precious manna down.
Israel saw it on the ground;
It was the God who now provides for me.

"Here I May Be Weak and Poor"
by Charles Albert Tindley, 1905
(author's adaptation)

Refrain:
Feed the hungry,
    and help those in trouble.
Then your light will shine out from the darkness,
    and the darkness around you will be as bright as noon.

Isaiah 58:10

The Lord's Prayer:
Our Father, who art in heaven,
Hallowed be thy name.
Thy kingdom come,
Thy will be done on earth,
As it is in heaven.
Give us this day our daily bread.
And forgive us our sins, as we forgive those who sin against us.
And lead us not into temptation, but deliver us from evil.
For thine is the kingdom, and the power, and the glory,
forever and ever.

Today's Prayer:
I thank you that you do not require us to be serious all the time. Thank you that you do not call us to a life of unending work. I thank you for the gift of fun, the gift of laughter, the gift of recreation. Help me to learn to follow your Spirit into the moments when I can let go of the list of things to be done and rest, relax, and play. Show me how to be aware of your presence in those times today. Fill my fun with your Spirit.

Concluding Prayer:
Creator of giraffes and duck-billed platypi I praise you for your sense of humor and the gift of fun. As I move from the middle of this day to its end, give me fun. Give me laughter. Open my eyes to see the hilarious gifts you are giving me along my way. Even as the day draws on and my heart is tempted to sadness and stress, give me the courage to find something to laugh about even in the middle of the reality of my life. Lord, give me fun. *Amen.*

AFTERNOON PRAYER

Call to Prayer:
Whatever is good and perfect comes down to us from God our
Father, who created all the lights in the heavens. He never changes or
casts a shifting shadow.

James 1:17

Confession:
Yes, I have sinned.
I have disobeyed your instructions and commands,
    Because I was afraid of the people around me
        of what they would think
        of what they would say
        of what they would do.
Instead of following you, instead of living a holy life,
    I did what they wanted.
    I let go and was swept away in the stream of their expectations.
But now, please forgive my sin.
    Open my eyes to see who I can surround myself with that will
lead me to you.

1 Samuel 15:24-25
(author's paraphrase of NLT)

Invitation:
Now I come ready to hear you speak,
    For your voice is sweet
    And your face is lovely.
Let me hear.
Let me see.

Refrain:
We put our hope in the LORD.
    He is our help and our shield.
In him our hearts rejoice,
    for we trust in his holy name.

Psalm 33:20-21

Reading:

As Jesus and the disciples approached Jerusalem, they came to the town of Bethphage on the Mount of Olives. Jesus sent two of them on ahead. "Go into the village over there," he said. "As soon as you enter it, you will see a donkey tied there, with its colt beside it. Untie them and bring them to me. If anyone asks what you are doing, just say, 'The Lord needs them,' and he will immediately let you take them."

This took place to fulfill the prophecy that said,

"Tell the people of Jerusalem,
'Look, your King is coming to you.
He is humble, riding on a donkey—
riding on a donkey's colt.' "

The two disciples did as Jesus commanded. They brought the donkey and the colt to him and threw their garments over the colt, and he sat on it.

Most of the crowd spread their garments on the road ahead of him, and others cut branches from the trees and spread them on the road. Jesus was in the center of the procession, and the people all around him were shouting,

"Praise God for the Son of David!
Blessings on the one who comes in the name of the LORD!
Praise God in highest heaven!"

The entire city of Jerusalem was in an uproar as he entered. "Who is this?" they asked.

And the crowds replied, "It's Jesus, the prophet from Nazareth in Galilee."

Matthew 21:1-11

Refrain:

We put our hope in the LORD.
He is our help and our shield.
In him our hearts rejoice,
for we trust in his holy name.

Psalm 33:20-21

Psalm:

I will exalt you, LORD, for you rescued me.
  You refused to let my enemies triumph over me.
O LORD my God, I cried to you for help,
  and you restored my health.
You brought me up from the grave, O LORD.
  You kept me from falling into the pit of death.
Sing to the LORD, all you godly ones!
  Praise his holy name.
For his anger lasts only a moment,
  but his favor lasts a lifetime!
Weeping may last through the night,
  but joy comes with the morning.
When I was prosperous, I said,
  "Nothing can stop me now!"
Your favor, O LORD, made me as secure as a mountain.
  Then you turned away from me, and I was shattered.
I cried out to you, O LORD.
  I begged the Lord for mercy, saying,
"What will you gain if I die,
  if I sink into the grave?
Can my dust praise you?
  Can it tell of your faithfulness?
Hear me, LORD, and have mercy on me.
  Help me, O LORD."
You have turned my mourning into joyful dancing.
  You have taken away my clothes of mourning and clothed me
with joy, that I might sing praises to you and not be silent.
  O LORD my God, I will give you thanks forever!

Psalm 30

Refrain:

We put our hope in the LORD.
  He is our help and our shield.
In him our hearts rejoice,
  for we trust in his holy name.

Psalm 33:20-21

The Lord's Prayer:

Our Father, who art in heaven,
Hallowed be thy name.
Thy kingdom come,
Thy will be done on earth,
As it is in heaven.
Give us this day our daily bread.
And forgive us our sins, as we forgive those who sin against us.
And lead us not into temptation, but deliver us from evil.
For thine is the kingdom, and the power, and the glory,
forever and ever.

Today's Prayer:

I thank you that you do not require us to be serious all the time. Thank you that you do not call us to a life of unending work. I thank you for the gift of fun, the gift of laughter, the gift of recreation. Help me to learn to follow your Spirit into the moments when I can let go of the list of things to be done and rest, relax, and play. Show me how to be aware of your presence in those times today. Fill my fun with your Spirit.

Concluding Prayer:

As the sun begins to set, and the color of its light fades from white to orange, I see that nothing lasts forever. Everything has a dawn, and everything has an afternoon that leads to evening. Show me now the afternoon and evening things in my life. Show me those things that are on their way out and let me celebrate the good things that came because of them. Then, give me the strength to let them go. Give me the courage to resist the temptation to hold on to them too long; rather, let me embrace the way their ending makes way for a new beginning. *Amen.*

END OF DAY PRAYER

Call to Prayer:
May the Lord Almighty grant me and those I love a peaceful night and a perfect end.

from The Book of Common Prayer

Confession:
Most merciful God,
I confess that I have sinned against you
in thought, word, and deed,
by what I have done
and by what I have left undone.
I have not loved you with my whole heart;
I have not loved my neighbors as myself.
I am truly sorry and I humbly repent.
For the sake of your Son Jesus Christ,
have mercy on me and forgive me,
that I may delight in you will
and walk in your ways,
to the glory of your name.

from The Book of Common Prayer

Invitation:
So the Word became human and made his home among us. He was full of unfailing love and faithfulness. And we have seen his glory, the glory of the Father's one and only Son.

John 1:14

Refrain:
Stay alert! Watch out for your great enemy, the devil. He prowls around like a roaring lion, looking for someone to devour. Stand firm against him, and be strong in your faith. Remember that your Christian brothers and sisters all over the world are going through the same kind of suffering you are.

1 Peter 5:8-9

Reading:

For the kingdom of heaven is like the landowner who went out early one morning to hire workers for his vineyard. He agreed to pay the normal daily wage and sent them out to work.

At nine o'clock in the morning he was passing through the marketplace and saw some people standing around doing nothing. So he hired them, telling them he would pay them whatever was right at the end of the day. So they went to work in the vineyard. At noon and again at three o'clock he did the same thing.

At five o'clock that afternoon he was in town again and saw some more people standing around. He asked them, "Why haven't you been working today?"

They replied, "Because no one hired us." The landowner told them, "Then go out and join the others in my vineyard."

That evening he told the foreman to call the workers in and pay them, beginning with the last workers first. When those hired at five o'clock were paid, each received a full day's wage. When those hired first came to get their pay, they assumed they would receive more. But they, too, were paid a day's wage. When they received their pay, they protested to the owner, "Those people worked only one hour, and yet you've paid them just as much as you paid us who worked all day in the scorching heat."

He answered one of them, "Friend, I haven't been unfair! Didn't you agree to work all day for the usual wage? Take your money and go. I wanted to pay this last worker the same as you. Is it against the law for me to do what I want with my money? Should you be jealous because I am kind to others?"

So those who are last now will be first then, and those who are first will be last.

Matthew 20:1-16

Refrain:

Stay alert! Watch out for your great enemy, the devil. He prowls around like a roaring lion, looking for someone to devour. Stand firm against him, and be strong in your faith. Remember that your Christian brothers and sisters all over the world are going through the same kind of suffering you are.

1 Peter 5:8-9

Psalm:

When the pathway of duty seems danger filled,
And the charms of worldly beauty almost win my feeble will,
While I see the Cross uplifted, and can hear the King's command,
I will go, if my Father holds my hand.

I will go, I will go,
Though the mountains are high and the valleys low.
I will go, I will go,
I will go if my Father holds my hand.

If my Father holds my hand, I can keep the narrow way.
If my Father holds my hand, I can never go astray.
Though often it is so dark I can hardly find the way,
I will go, if my Father holds my hand.

I will go, I will go,
Though the mountains are high and the valleys low.
I will go, I will go,
I will go if my Father holds my hand.

Though my strength is weak, by his grace I will seek
To rest like Mary at the Savior's feet,
Then to climb to the heights of the pure delight.
I will go, if my Father holds my hand.

I will go, I will go,
Though the mountains are high and the valleys low.
I will go, I will go,
I will go if my Father holds my hand.

When in the vale of sorrow I am called to go,
And it seems each tomorrow simply brings another woe,
I am satisfied to follow where he leads, this I know.
I will go, if my Father holds my hand.

I will go, I will go,
Though the mountains are high and the valleys low.

I will go, I will go,
I will go if my Father holds my hand.

When the awful waves of Jordan beat upon my soul,
In the icy hands of death my limbs are growing cold,
I have nothing then to fear if my Lord is near.
I will go, if my Father holds my hand.

"I Will Go, If My Father Holds My Hand"
by Charles Albert Tindley, 1907
(author's adaptation)

Refrain:

Stay alert! Watch out for your great enemy, the devil. He prowls around like a roaring lion, looking for someone to devour. Stand firm against him, and be strong in your faith. Remember that your Christian brothers and sisters all over the world are going through the same kind of suffering you are.

1 Peter 5:8-9

The Lord's Prayer:

Our Father, who art in heaven,
Hallowed be thy name.
Thy kingdom come,
Thy will be done on earth,
As it is in heaven.
Give us this day our daily bread.
And forgive us our sins, as we forgive those who sin against us.
And lead us not into temptation, but deliver us from evil.
For thine is the kingdom, and the power, and the glory,
forever and ever.

Today's Prayer:

I thank you that you do not require us to be serious all the time. Thank you that you do not call us to a life of unending work. I thank you for the gift of fun, the gift of laughter, the gift of recreation. Help me to learn to follow your Spirit into the moments when I can let go of the list of things to be done and rest, relax, and play. Show me how to be aware of your presence in those times today. Fill my fun with your Spirit.

Concluding Prayer:

Night is here, and my day is done. I pray that as I sleep you will keep me safe and give me wondrous dreams to fill my night with the light of the glorious future you have for me. Help me to see you, even though I sleep, and to experience the rest that you took on the seventh day. Use this night to replenish my body and let me wake rested and ready to serve you in a new day tomorrow. *Amen.*

MIDNIGHT PRAYER

Call to Prayer:
I could ask the darkness to hide me
and the light around me to become night—
but even in darkness I cannot hide from you.
To you the night shines as bright as day.
Darkness and light are the same to you.

Psalm 139:11-12

Invitation:
In the middle of the night I rise to hear you speak,
For your words bring light even in the darkest nights.

Refrain:
Darkness as black as night covers all the nations of the earth,
but the glory of the LORD rises and appears over you.

Isaiah 60:2

Reading:
In the sixth month of Elizabeth's pregnancy, God sent the angel Gabriel to Nazareth, a village in Galilee, to a virgin named Mary. She was engaged to be married to a man named Joseph, a descendant of King David. Gabriel appeared to her and said, "Greetings, favored woman! The Lord is with you!"

Confused and disturbed, Mary tried to think what the angel could mean. "Don't be afraid, Mary," the angel told her, "for you have found favor with God! You will conceive and give birth to a son, and you will name him Jesus. He will be very great and will be called the Son of the Most High. The Lord God will give him the throne of his ancestor David. And he will reign over Israel forever; his kingdom will never end!"

Mary asked the angel, "But how can this happen? I am a virgin."

The angel replied, "The Holy Spirit will come upon you, and the power of the Most High will overshadow you. So the baby to be born will be holy, and he will be called the Son of God. What's more, your relative Elizabeth has become pregnant in her old age! People used to say she was barren, but she has conceived a son and is now in her sixth month. For nothing is impossible with God."

Mary responded, "I am the Lord's servant. May everything you have said about me come true." And then the angel left her.

Luke 1:26-38

Refrain:
Darkness as black as night covers all the nations of the earth,
    but the glory of the LORD rises and appears over you.

Isaiah 60:2

Psalm:
Almighty God, you have given us grace at this time with one accord to make our common requests to you; and you have promised through your well-beloved Son that when two or three are gathered together in his name you will be in the midst of them: Fulfill now, O Lord, our desires and petitions as may be best for us, granting us in this world knowledge of your truth and in the age to come life everlasting.

Prayer of St. Chrysostom, circa 400 CE

Refrain:
Darkness as black as night covers all the nations of the earth,
    but the glory of the LORD rises and appears over you.

Isaiah 60:2

The Lord's Prayer:
Our Father, who art in heaven,
Hallowed be thy name.
Thy kingdom come,
Thy will be done on earth,
As it is in heaven.
Give us this day our daily bread.
And forgive us our sins, as we forgive those who sin against us.
And lead us not into temptation, but deliver us from evil.
For thine is the kingdom, and the power, and the glory,
forever and ever.

Today's Prayer:
I thank you that you do not require us to be serious all the time. Thank you that you do not call us to a life of unending work. I thank you for the gift of fun, the gift of laughter, the gift of recreation. Help me to learn to follow your Spirit into the moments when I can let go of the list of things to be done and rest, relax, and play. Show me how to be aware of your presence in those times today. Fill my fun with your Spirit.

Concluding Prayer:
In the darkest night, you are there. In the hardest times of my life, you have been there. As I return to the land of sleep and rest, let me rest in your presence. Let my soul be filled with your Spirit as my body recovers from this day. When I wake tomorrow, may I know from the beginning that you are there. May my eyes open knowing that your Spirit is present with me. *Amen.*

SUNDAY

DAWN PRAYER

Call to Prayer:
I awake with the rays of dawn to your holy mysteries.

Invitation:
I long for the Lord
    more than sentries long for the dawn,
    yes, more than sentries long for the dawn.

Psalm 130:6

Refrain:
But let me reveal to you a wonderful secret. We will not all die, but we will all be transformed!

1 Corinthians 15:51

Reading:
Can you solve the mysteries of God?
    Can you discover everything about the Almighty?
Such knowledge is higher than the heavens—
    and who are you?
It is deeper than the underworld—
    what do you know?
It is broader than the earth
    and wider than the sea.
If God comes and puts a person in prison
    or calls the court to order, who can stop him?
For he knows those who are false,
    and he takes note of all their sins.
An empty-headed person won't become wise
    any more than a wild donkey can bear a human child.
If only you would prepare your heart
    and lift up your hands to him in prayer!
Get rid of your sins,
    and leave all iniquity behind you.
Then your face will brighten with innocence.
    You will be strong and free of fear.

You will forget your misery;
　　it will be like water flowing away.
Your life will be brighter than the noonday.
　　Even darkness will be as bright as morning.
Having hope will give you courage.
　　You will be protected and will rest in safety.
You will lie down unafraid,
　　and many will look to you for help.
But the wicked will be blinded.
　　They will have no escape.
　　Their only hope is death.

Job 11:7-20

Refrain:

But let me reveal to you a wonderful secret. We will not all die, but we will all be transformed!

1 Corinthians 15:51

Psalm:

You great, mysterious, God unknown,
Whose love has gently led me on
Even from my infant days;
My inmost soul expose to view,
And tell me if I ever knew
Your justifying grace.

If I have only known your fear,
And followed with a heart sincere
Your drawing from above,
Now, now transforming grace bestow,
And let my sprinkled conscience know
Thy sweet forgiving love.

Short of your love I would not stop,
A stranger to the gospel hope,
The sense of sin forgiven;
I would not, Lord, my soul deceive,
Without your inward witness live,

That foretaste of heaven.

If now the witness were in me,
Would testify of you to me,
In Jesus reconciled?
And should I not with faith draw nigh,
And boldly, Abba Father, cry,
I know myself your child?

Ah! Never let your servant rest,
Till, of my part in Christ possessed,
I on your mercy feed.
Unworthy of the crumbs that fall,
Yet raised by him who died for all,
To eat the children's bread.

Whatever blocks your pardoning love,
Or sin, or righteousness, remove,
Your glory to display;
My heart of unbelief convince,
And now absolve me from my sins,
And take them all away.

"Thou Great, Mysterious God Unknown"
By Charles Wesley, 1700s
(author's adaptation)

Refrain:
But let me reveal to you a wonderful secret. We will not all die, but we will all be transformed!

1 Corinthians 15:51

The Lord's Prayer:
Our Father, who art in heaven,
Hallowed be thy name.
Thy kingdom come,
Thy will be done on earth,
As it is in heaven.
Give us this day our daily bread.
And forgive us our sins, as we forgive those who sin against us.

And lead us not into temptation, but deliver us from evil.
For thine is the kingdom, and the power, and the glory,
forever and ever.

Today's Prayer:

This Sabbath day, this holy gift of worship and rest, give me the
miracle of time. Make the things that come up, that seek to tempt me
away from resting in your presence today, be so unimportant that I
can let them go until this day ends. May the people who drain me
of physical and emotional energy not have any pressing need that
cannot wait until tomorrow for a response. Give me the gift of time
and the courage to fill it with rest, enjoyment, and relaxation.

Concluding Prayer:

I cannot come close to completely understanding you, and I am so
grateful that is the case. I am thankful that you are so powerful and
unpredictable that I simply stand in awe when I consider what you
have done. And to think that I am counted among your creations!
What a wonderful gift! I praise you for your mystery. I praise you for
your secrets! I praise you for all that I do not yet know, and I praise
you for all that I will never know! As I begin the day in yet another
mysterious dawn, let me revel in the unknown and listen for your
whisper there. *Amen.*

MORNING PRAYER

Call to Prayer:
Many, LORD, are asking, "Who will bring us prosperity?"
> Let the light of your face shine on us.

Psalm 4:6 (NIV)

Confession:
Merciful God I have betrayed you
> By following my own way,
> By listening to myself over you,
> By turning a deaf ear to the voice of your Spirit,
> By speaking hate instead of love,
> By offering greed instead of generosity,
> By spreading gossip instead of kindness.

Forgive me.
> Because you love me with an everlasting love.
> Because you are working all things together for the good of those who love you.
> Because you sent your Son to live, die, and be resurrected for humanity.

Lord have mercy,
Christ have mercy,
Lord have mercy.

Invitation:
"Do not let your hearts be troubled. You believe in God; believe also in me.

John 14:1 (NIV)

Refrain:
For I am not ashamed of this Good News about Christ. It is the power of God at work, saving everyone who believes—the Jew first and also the Gentile.

Romans 1:16

Reading:

We believe in one God,
    the Father, the Almighty,
    maker of heaven and earth,
    of all that is, seen and unseen.

We believe in one Lord, Jesus Christ,
    the only Son of God,
    eternally begotten of the Father,
    God from God, Light from Light,
    true God from true God,
    begotten, not made,
    of one Being with the Father.
Through him all things were made.
For us and for our salvation
    he came down from heaven:
    by the power of the Holy Spirit
    he became incarnate from the Virgin Mary,
    and was made man.
For our sake he was crucified under Pontius Pilate;
    he suffered death and was buried.
On the third day he rose again
    in accordance with the Scriptures;
    he ascended into heaven
    and is seated at the right hand of the Father.
He will come again in glory to judge the living and the dead,
    and his kingdom will have no end.

We believe in the Holy Spirit, the Lord, the giver of life,
    who proceeds from the Father and the Son.
With the Father and the Son he is worshiped and glorified.
He has spoken through the Prophets.
We believe in one holy catholic and apostolic Church.
We acknowledge one baptism for the forgiveness of sins.
We look for the resurrection of the dead,
    and the life of the world to come.

Nicene Creed
325 CE

Refrain:

For I am not ashamed of this Good News about Christ. It is the power of God at work, saving everyone who believes—the Jew first and also the Gentile.

Romans 1:16

Psalm:

We are tossed and driven
on the restless sea of time;
somber skies and howling seas
often followed a bright sunshine;
in that land of perfect day,
when the mists are rolled away,
we will understand it better eventually.

Eventually, when the morning comes,
when the saints of God are gathered home,
we'll tell the story how we've overcome,
for we'll understand it better eventually.

We are often lacking
the things that life demands,
in need of food and want of shelter,
thirsty hills and barren lands;
we are trusting in the Lord,
and according to God's Word,
we will understand it better eventually.

Eventually, when the morning comes,
when the saints of God are gathered home,
we'll tell the story how we've overcome,
for we'll understand it better eventually.

Trials dark on every hand,
and we cannot understand
all the ways of God would lead us
to that blessed promised land;
but he guides us with his eye,

and we'll follow till we die,
for we'll understand it better eventually.

Eventually, when the morning comes,
when the saints of God are gathered home,
we'll tell the story how we've overcome,
for we'll understand it better eventually.

Temptations, hidden snares
often take us unawares,
and our hearts are made to bleed
for a thoughtless word or deed;
and we wonder why the test
when we try to do our best,
but we'll understand it better eventually.

"We'll Understand It Better By and By"
by Charles Albert Tindley, 1905
(author's adaptation)

Refrain:

For I am not ashamed of this Good News about Christ. It is the power of God at work, saving everyone who believes—the Jew first and also the Gentile.

Romans 1:16

The Lord's Prayer:

Our Father, who art in heaven,
Hallowed be thy name.
Thy kingdom come,
Thy will be done on earth,
As it is in heaven.
Give us this day our daily bread.
And forgive us our sins, as we forgive those who sin against us.
And lead us not into temptation, but deliver us from evil.
For thine is the kingdom, and the power, and the glory,
forever and ever.

Today's Prayer:

This Sabbath day, this holy gift of worship and rest, give me the miracle of time. Make the things that come up, that seek to tempt me away from resting in your presence today, be so unimportant that I can let them go until this day ends. May the people who drain me of physical and emotional energy not have any pressing need that cannot wait until tomorrow for a response. Give me the gift of time and the courage to fill it with rest, enjoyment, and relaxation.

Concluding Prayer:

This Sabbath morning, I stand with countless Christians. I stand with those who have long since passed away hundreds or thousands of years ago. I stand with those who have yet to be born. I stand up and say, "I Believe." I believe not because someone told me to, or because I feel that I have to, but because I know you. You have revealed yourself to me through people, through your Scriptures, through the mysteries of my own heart, and through the power of my logical mind. Today, in this moment, I believe. Now, help me with my unbelief. *Amen.*

NOONDAY PRAYER

Call to Prayer:
Praise the LORD who has given rest to his people Israel, just as he promised. Not one word has failed of all the wonderful promises he gave through his servant Moses.

1 Kings 8:56

Invitation:
My world is nonstop. My friends are nonstop.
    My family is nonstop. My school is nonstop.
But you give rest. You call me to rest.
    You make naps spiritual. Call me into your rest-giving arms.

Refrain:
Those who live in the shelter of the Most High
    will find rest in the shadow of the Almighty.
This I declare about the LORD:
    He alone is my refuge, my place of safety;
    he is my God, and I trust him.

Psalm 91:1-2

Psalm:
Will you come, will you come, with your poor broken heart,
Burdened and sin oppressed?
Lay it down at the feet of your Savior and Lord,
Jesus will give you rest.

O happy rest, sweet, happy rest.
Jesus will give you rest.
Oh! why won't you come in simple, trusting faith?
Jesus will give you rest.

Will you come, will you come? There is mercy for you,
Balm for your aching breast;
Only come as you are, and believe on his name,
Jesus will give you rest.

O happy rest, sweet, happy rest.
Jesus will give you rest.
Oh! Why won't you come in simple, trusting faith?
Jesus will give you rest.

Will you come, will you come? You have nothing to pay;
Jesus, who loves you best,
By his death on the cross purchased life for your soul.
Jesus will give you rest.

O happy rest, sweet, happy rest.
Jesus will give you rest.
Oh! Why won't you come in simple, trusting faith?
Jesus will give you rest.

Will you come, will you come? How he pleads with you now!
Fly to his loving breast;
And whatever your sin or your sorrow may be,
Jesus will give you rest.

O happy rest, sweet, happy rest.
Jesus will give you rest.
Oh! Why won't you come in simple, trusting faith?
Jesus will give you rest.

"Will You Come? (Jesus Will Give You Rest)"
by Fanny Crosby, 1889
(author's adaptation)

Refrain:
Those who live in the shelter of the Most High
    will find rest in the shadow of the Almighty.
This I declare about the LORD:
    He alone is my refuge, my place of safety;
    he is my God, and I trust him.

Psalm 91:1-2

The Lord's Prayer:
Our Father, who art in heaven,
Hallowed be thy name.
Thy kingdom come,
Thy will be done on earth,
As it is in heaven.
Give us this day our daily bread.
And forgive us our sins, as we forgive those who sin against us.
And lead us not into temptation, but deliver us from evil.
For thine is the kingdom, and the power, and the glory,
forever and ever.

Today's Prayer:
This Sabbath day, this holy gift of worship and rest, give me the
miracle of time. Make the things that come up, that seek to tempt me
away from resting in your presence today, be so unimportant that I
can let them go until this day ends. May the people who drain me
of physical and emotional energy not have any pressing need that
cannot wait until tomorrow for a response. Give me the gift of time
and the courage to fill it with rest, enjoyment, and relaxation.

Concluding Prayer:
I can wear myself out even on the weekends, even on Sundays when
I should be resting. While I confess that I don't rest as much as you
call me to, I pray that as noon fades into afternoon and evening, you
would give me enough confidence in what is happening to let go of
some of my tasks and schedule so that I can rest. Would you help me
even put down some entertainment, wind down, and be quiet for a
moment in my noisy world? Give me rest, Lord. *Amen.*

AFTERNOON PRAYER

Call to Prayer:
Blessed are all those
>who are careful to do this.
>>Blessed are those who honor my Sabbath days of rest
>>and keep themselves from doing wrong.

Isaiah 56:2

Confession
I have sinned. I have made mistakes. I have messed up.
>I have broken your law;
>I have rebelled against your love;
>I have hurt my friends;
>I have lied to those I love;
>I have ignored those in need right here in my city;
>I have turned a blind eye to those in need all over the world.

Forgive me, I pray.
>Free me from the weight of my sin that keeps my feet on the ground,
>That keeps me from ascending to the heavens.
>Bring back to me the joy of my salvation
>That I may live with your forever.

Invitation:
Keep the Sabbath day holy.
>>Don't pursue your own interests on that day,
>but enjoy the Sabbath
>>and speak of it with delight as the LORD's holy day.
>Honor the Sabbath in everything you do on that day,
>>and don't follow your own desires or talk idly.

Then the LORD will be your delight.
>>I will give you great honor
>and satisfy you with the inheritance I promised to your ancestor
Jacob.
>>I, the LORD, have spoken!

Isaiah 58:13-14

Refrain:

And I gave them my Sabbath days of rest as a sign between them and me. It was to remind them that I am the LORD, who had set them apart to be holy.

Ezekiel 20:12

Reading:

One Sabbath day as Jesus was walking through some grainfields, his disciples began breaking off heads of grain to eat. But the Pharisees said to Jesus, "Look, why are they breaking the law by harvesting grain on the Sabbath?"

Jesus said to them, "Haven't you ever read in the Scriptures what David did when he and his companions were hungry? He went into the house of God (during the days when Abiathar was high priest) and broke the law by eating the sacred loaves of bread that only the priests are allowed to eat. He also gave some to his companions."

Then Jesus said to them, "The Sabbath was made to meet the needs of people, and not people to meet the requirements of the Sabbath. So the Son of Man is Lord, even over the Sabbath!"

Jesus went into the synagogue again and noticed a man with a deformed hand. Since it was the Sabbath, Jesus' enemies watched him closely. If he healed the man's hand, they planned to accuse him of working on the Sabbath.

Jesus said to the man with the deformed hand, "Come and stand in front of everyone." Then he turned to his critics and asked, "Does the law permit good deeds on the Sabbath, or is it a day for doing evil? Is this a day to save life or to destroy it?" But they wouldn't answer him.

He looked around at them angrily and was deeply saddened by their hard hearts. Then he said to the man, "Hold out your hand." So the man held out his hand, and it was restored! At once the Pharisees went away and met with the supporters of Herod to plot how to kill Jesus.

Mark 2:23-3:6

Refrain:
And I gave them my Sabbath days of rest as a sign between them and
me. It was to remind them that I am the LORD, who had set them
apart to be holy.

Ezekiel 20:12

Psalm:
It is good to give thanks to the LORD,
to sing praises to the Most High.
It is good to proclaim your unfailing love in the morning,
your faithfulness in the evening,
accompanied by the ten-stringed harp
and the melody of the lyre.

You thrill me, LORD, with all you have done for me!
I sing for joy because of what you have done.
O LORD, what great works you do!
And how deep are your thoughts.
Only a simpleton would not know,
and only a fool would not understand this:
Though the wicked sprout like weeds
and evildoers flourish,
they will be destroyed forever.

But you, O LORD, will be exalted forever.
Your enemies, LORD, will surely perish;
all evildoers will be scattered.
But you have made me as strong as a wild ox.
You have anointed me with the finest oil.
My eyes have seen the downfall of my enemies;
my ears have heard the defeat of my wicked opponents.
But the godly will flourish like palm trees
and grow strong like the cedars of Lebanon.
For they are transplanted to the LORD's own house.
They flourish in the courts of our God.
Even in old age they will still produce fruit;
they will remain vital and green.
They will declare, "The LORD is just!

He is my rock!
There is no evil in him!"

Psalm 92

Refrain:
And I gave them my Sabbath days of rest as a sign between them and
me. It was to remind them that I am the LORD, who had set them
apart to be holy.

Ezekiel 20:12

The Lord's Prayer:
Our Father, who art in heaven,
Hallowed be thy name.
Thy kingdom come,
Thy will be done on earth,
As it is in heaven.
Give us this day our daily bread.
And forgive us our sins, as we forgive those who sin against us.
And lead us not into temptation, but deliver us from evil.
For thine is the kingdom, and the power, and the glory,
forever and ever.

Today's Prayer:
This Sabbath day, this holy gift of worship and rest, give me the
miracle of time. Make the things that come up, that seek to tempt me
away from resting in your presence today, be so unimportant that I
can let them go until this day ends. May the people who drain me
of physical and emotional energy not have any pressing need that
cannot wait until tomorrow for a response. Give me the gift of time
and the courage to fill it with rest, enjoyment, and relaxation.

Concluding Prayer:
I thank you for calling us to rest. I thank you that you do not define
my value to you or to your kingdom based on how much work I can
accomplish. Yet, the rest of the world often evaluates me much more
like a machine than like a person. God, help me let go of the world's
pressure to define my worth like a machine, deciding how good I am
based on how much I can produce. Instead, let me find my value in

your eyes as you see within me what I often cannot see myself: the image of God. Give me grace to accept your loving, caring, highly-valued perception of me over any other perception. *Amen.*

END OF DAY PRAYER

Call to Prayer:
May the Lord Almighty grant me and those I love a peaceful night
and a perfect end.

from The Book of Common Prayer

Confession:
As I end this Sabbath day, I bring you a simple confession:
I have sinned.
In your unending mercy, forgive me.

Invitation:
Answer me when I call to you,
O God who declares me innocent.
Free me from my troubles.
Have mercy on me and hear my prayer.

Psalm 4:1

Refrain:
O LORD, I have come to you for protection;
don't let me be disgraced.
Save me, for you do what is right.

Psalm 31:1

Reading:
At that time Jesus prayed this prayer: "O Father, Lord of heaven
and earth, thank you for hiding these things from those who think
themselves wise and clever, and for revealing them to the childlike.
Yes, Father, it pleased you to do it this way!

"My Father has entrusted everything to me. No one truly knows
the Son except the Father, and no one truly knows the Father except
the Son and those to whom the Son chooses to reveal him."

Then Jesus said, "Come to me, all of you who are weary and carry
heavy burdens, and I will give you rest. Take my yoke upon you. Let
me teach you, because I am humble and gentle at heart, and you will
find rest for your souls. For my yoke is easy to bear, and the burden I

give you is light."

Matthew 11:25-30

Refrain:

O LORD, I have come to you for protection;
    don't let me be disgraced.
    Save me, for you do what is right.

Psalm 31:1

Psalm:

Lord, make me an instrument of your peace;
Where there is hatred, let me sow love;
Where there is injury, pardon;
Where there is doubt, faith;
Where there is despair, hope;
Where there is darkness, light;
And where there is sadness, joy.

O Divine Master,
Grant that I may not so much seek
To be consoled as to console;
To be understood, as to understand;
To be loved, as to love;
For it is in giving that we receive,
It is in pardoning that we are pardoned,
And it is in dying that we are born to eternal life.

"Prayer of Saint Francis"
Attributed to Francis of Assisi, 1181-1226

Refrain:

O LORD, I have come to you for protection;
    don't let me be disgraced.
    Save me, for you do what is right.

Psalm 31:1

The Lord's Prayer:
Our Father, who art in heaven,
Hallowed be thy name.
Thy kingdom come,
Thy will be done on earth,
As it is in heaven.
Give us this day our daily bread.
And forgive us our sins, as we forgive those who sin against us.
And lead us not into temptation, but deliver us from evil.
For thine is the kingdom, and the power, and the glory,
forever and ever.

Today's Prayer:
This Sabbath day, this holy gift of worship and rest, give me the miracle of time. Make the things that come up, that seek to tempt me away from resting in your presence today, be so unimportant that I can let them go until this day ends. May the people who drain me of physical and emotional energy not have any pressing need that cannot wait until tomorrow for a response. Give me the gift of time and the courage to fill it with rest, enjoyment, and relaxation.

Concluding Prayer:
Be present, O merciful God, and protect us through the hours of this night, so that we who are wearied by the changes and chances of this life may rest in your eternal changelessness; through Jesus Christ our Lord. *Amen.*

from *The Book of Common Prayer*

MIDNIGHT PRAYER

Call to Prayer:

The LORD rescues the godly;
> he is their fortress in times of trouble.

Psalm 37:39

Invitation:

Never let loyalty and kindness leave you!
> Tie them around your neck as a reminder.
> Write them deep within your heart.
Then you will find favor with both God and people,
> and you will earn a good reputation.

Proverbs 3:3-4

Refrain:

Put your hope in the LORD.
> Travel steadily along his path.

Psalm 37:34a

Reading:

O LORD, don't rebuke me in your anger
> or discipline me in your rage.
Have compassion on me, LORD, for I am weak.
> Heal me, LORD, for my bones are in agony.
I am sick at heart.
> How long, O LORD, until you restore me?

Return, O LORD, and rescue me.
> Save me because of your unfailing love.
For the dead do not remember you.
> Who can praise you from the grave?

I am worn out from sobbing.
> All night I flood my bed with weeping,
> drenching it with my tears.
My vision is blurred by grief;

my eyes are worn out because of all my enemies.

Go away, all you who do evil,
>   for the LORD has heard my weeping.
The LORD has heard my plea;
>   the LORD will answer my prayer.
May all my enemies be disgraced and terrified.
>   May they suddenly turn back in shame.

Psalm 6

Refrain:
Put your hope in the LORD.
>   Travel steadily along his path.

Psalm 37:34a

Psalm:
O Christ, our hope, our heart's desire,
redemption's only spring,
Creator of the world art you,
its Savior and its King.

How vast the mercy and the love,
which laid our sins on you
and led thee to a cruel death
to set thy people free.

But now the bands of death are burst,
the ransom has been paid;
and you are on thy Father's throne,
in glorious robes arrayed.

O Christ, be thou our lasting joy,
our ever great reward;
our only glory may it be
to glory in the Lord!

All praise to you, ascended Lord;
all glory ever be

to Father, Son, and Spirit blest
through all eternity.

"O Christ, Our Hope, Our Heart's Desire"
by John Chandler, 1837
(author's adaptation)

Refrain:

Put your hope in the LORD.
    Travel steadily along his path.

Psalm 37:34a

The Lord's Prayer:

Our Father, who art in heaven,
Hallowed be thy name.
Thy kingdom come,
Thy will be done on earth,
As it is in heaven.
Give us this day our daily bread.
And forgive us our sins, as we forgive those who sin against us.
And lead us not into temptation, but deliver us from evil.
For thine is the kingdom, and the power, and the glory, forever and
ever.

Today's Prayer:

This Sabbath day, this holy gift of worship and rest, give me the
miracle of time. Make the things that come up, that seek to tempt me
away from resting in your presence today, be so unimportant that I
can let them go until this day ends. May the people who drain me
of physical and emotional energy not have any pressing need that
cannot wait until tomorrow for a response. Give me the gift of time
and the courage to fill it with rest, enjoyment, and relaxation.

Concluding Prayer:

As I climb into bed I thank you for another day and another night
with you. I thank you for calling me to rest. Now, let me be renewed
as I sleep and made ready for what lies ahead that my life may be a
beacon of hope for my world. May this night's rest give me what I
need to minister tomorrow. *Amen.*

RIGHT WORDS
FOR THE RIGHT TIME

RIGHT WORDS FOR THE RIGHT TIME
(PRAYERS FOR EVERY OCCASION)

FOR DAILY LIVING

Cleaning a Room:

God of the universe, when I look at all that you made, I can see that when you create, you do so with organization and order. Because you tilted the earth precisely, we have seasons and tides. The more I learn about the human body, the more amazed I am at how detailed you are. As I organize and bring this room back into order, help me think about your creation. Help cleaning this room become an act of worship for me. Help me be able to see my picking up laundry and vacuuming as a way to make my environment a reflection of who you are. *Amen.*

Coffee:

Hallelujah! Praise be the God of Abraham, Isaac, and Jacob—the Creator of heaven and earth and coffee. Okay, I know that may be overblown, but seriously. *Coffee.* Thanks for that. Thanks for the way holding the warm cup in my hands gives me the sense of peace and how smelling the steam as it rises from the cup seems to bring light to the darkest of mornings. Thank you for creating things like coffee beans that seem to be nothing more than a gift for humanity. Thank you, God, for coffee. *Amen.*

Food:

Lord Jesus, my Provider, thank you for the food I have to eat. I thank you for creating a world that produces enough for all its inhabitants to have enough, even if we have not yet figured out how to work together to make that happen. Which brings me to my next thought: I must ask for your forgiveness. Forgive me for the ways in which I participate in a system that causes people to die of hunger while food rots away in landfills. Forgive me for the times I am ungrateful for the food that is in front of me. As I consume a physical representation of your provision, give me the grace to see how the food connects me to everything and everyone. Let me see eating as a spiritual endeavor.

Allow me to feel your faithfulness as I eat the food that sustains my body. *Amen.*

Video Games:

Thank you, God, for video games. I thank you for the ability to get drawn into someone else's imagination and lose myself in these creative distractions. I thank you for allowing me to live in such luxury that I can spend my time on pure entertainment. I pray that you would allow me to use this gift wisely. I pray that it would help me release tension and relax but would not isolate me and consume all my spare time—give me the discipline to not allow it to. Let me revel in the creativity of the game designers and developers and take full advantage of this wonderful gift: video games. *Amen.*

FOR SCHOOL

Beginning of the School Year:

We've done this before, God. We've started the school year together, and sometimes we've finished it together, though sometimes I feel like I leave you behind about half way through it. At the beginning of this new year, give me eyes to see the potential it contains: all of the opportunities ahead of me to grow and learn and minister to the people in my school. As I begin, I ask that you would give me an awareness of your presence as well as an awareness of the fact that I'm a physical expression of your presence everywhere I am in my school. Can you help me to see all the people there as your precious creations? Can you show me how I might be an agent of your grace and peace with friends, "enemies," teachers, administration, coaches, janitors, and aids? Will you so fill me with your light that my school becomes a more loving, peace-filled place because I am in it? And, when times get tough, surround me with people who speak words of truth, life, and godly support. Even when I fail and sin against you, use your Holy Spirit to make me aware of my sin. Give me the courage to ask for forgiveness and leave my sinful ways behind so that this year, I end my year where I am beginning it: with you. *Amen.*

Homework:

How long, oh Lord, will this homework last? How long will I be stuck in a moment between learning and knowing? How long must I endure this boring, long work? Here's what I need. I need you to somehow, transform this work from mind-numbing and boring to interesting and useful. Help me to find you in between the equations and definitions. And make the time I spend on this task feel like it's passing more quickly than it does. *Amen.*

Making a Good Grade:

It happened! I made the grade! I thank you for all that you have done to bring me to this point. I thank you for allowing me to participate in life and enjoy success well earned. Even in this moment of happiness, help me to learn to see every good gift (even this grade) as coming from you. Then, rejoice with me, sing with me, do a silly dance with me, and let me channel this win into a commitment to the work needed for another. *Amen.*

Before a Big Test:

There is a lot riding on this test, God. You know that already. It's just important for me to say that, because I really need this to go well. I know there's more I could have done to prepare (there is always more), but I feel I have a good shot at making the score I need. However, I know there is so much that can get in the way when the pressure is on. So, God, will you help me out? I need to be calm. I need to be able to focus on what is in front of me, and I need to remember the right answers. The ones I already know. I'm not asking you to magically make me have a perfect score (though I'm totally okay with that, btw). I'm asking you to give me the peace and focus I need to do well, to do my best. So, in your mercy, hear my prayer for this test. *Amen.*

History:

So many have come before me, and so many will come after me. But if it weren't for history, I wouldn't get to learn from those who came before and no one would be able to learn from what we are doing and discovering right now. So, Lord, thanks for history and for historians and all my history teachers too. Thank you for those who dive deep into the past and spend hours poring over ancient documents in libraries just so that we might learn from other generations' innovations and battles and successes and mistakes. Don't let me waste this incredible gift! Give me the hunger to learn from the past so that my future may be brighter. Thank you, God, for history! *Amen.*

Math:

You, O God, are the author of math. Whoa. As the universe expands and the planets spin and orbit around their stars, they all find a beautiful order—one that is perfectly reflected in equations. Through this gift you have given us the ability to stretch far beyond the limits of our own brains and create computers and smartphones and a world of other expressions of math that have really changed how we do virtually everything now and opened brilliant possibilities for the future. Bless the mathematicians, Lord. Inspire them, wake them in the middle of the night with solutions. And use them to make earth a better place for your people. *Amen.*

Science:

From the beginning you created science. As you gave the first human the task of naming all the animals, you actually created the entire field of taxonomy (and thank you for the science teacher who taught me what that was—or for the creators of the Internet, because I'm about to look it up). You called us from the beginning to care for and understand your creation, our planet, our universe. And since then, you have poured out so many gifts on our world and on me, over and over again through scientists' brains and the resources and scientific laws you put in this universe of ours. Thank you for vaccines and antibiotics. Thank you for satellites and GPS and the theory of relativity and the magnificence of chemistry, even if sometimes these things just blow my mind. Thank you for scientists like Bill Nye and Albert Einstein and Stephen Hawking. Thank you for those that help us understand the human body and the human mind, for those that help us grow the food we eat and care for the fish in the sea. Thank you, God, for science. *Amen.*

Group Project:

My grade is in someone else's hands. Actually, it's in the hands of more than one person. Though I'd like to think it's safe in their hands, I know it's not. I know that far too often someone has dropped the ball on me in one of these things. When that hasn't happened, someone else has had a life issue that has caused them to do a poor job or nothing at all. I know I've been the problem before too. So, forgive me for when I have dropped the ball in the past, give me grace to not drop it this time, and give me the miracle of a successful group project. *Amen.*

FOR FRIENDSHIPS

New Friendships:

Almighty and all-loving God, I thank you for the new friendship that is emerging in my life right now, and I thank you for the gift of all the friends that you have blessed me with in the past. I thank you for how growing closer to people helps me grow closer to you, and I thank you for the opportunities that friendship gives to be a support and be supported by others. I pray for this new friendship that you would give me the ability to be my true self as we begin, that the pieces I share are an accurate sample of who I really am. As I learn about this new friend, help me to see the beauty that you created inside him/her. As we share pieces of our own brokenness, help me to be kind in my reaction and help my new friend's reactions to be kind also. May the friend-love I experience in this relationship not only lead me closer to this person but lead me closer to you my Master, Savior, and Friend. *Amen.*

Betrayal by a Friend:

I am burning inside, God. It's good that I'm not as powerful as you are, because I would use my almightiness for revenge. I've had a trust betrayed and have lost hope in the world. How could someone I cared for so much treat me so horribly? I would ask you to, like, rain down frogs on them or something, but I know you love them too. (But, if you would like to do the frog thing I'm totally okay with that in this moment.) Can you help me heal? Can you help me trust? And can you teach me how to know who in this world can be trusted? For now, when I have lost trust in everyone else, I put my trust in you. Care for me and keep me safe as I listen to your voice sing sweet songs of healing to my aching soul. *Amen.*

Being Tempted Around Friends:

Why, O God, do I care so much about what other people think of me? Why is it that when I am around certain people at the wrong time, I end up completely walking away from what I know is right? Because that's the problem. I know what is right and I know what is wrong. When I really think about it, when I pray about it, I truly want to do what is right. I want to do what you want me to do. Why then do I constantly find myself doing what is wrong? Especially when I'm with these friends? I know my parents would tell me to ditch them because they aren't a good influence, but you and I both know that is way harder than it sounds. Can we start with me? Can you help me out? Will you fill me with your Spirit and give me strength to stand up under the temptation? And in the situations where it seems like it's too strong, will you show me a way out of the situation? Then, and this is the important part, give me the courage to take the way out you offer me? And, if I cannot follow you with these friends, help me find a new group of friends who will pressure me in a good way: to do the right things. *Amen.*

FOR DATING RELATIONSHIPS

After the Breakup:

It hurts. Not long ago I was so glad to experience the warmth of love and the passion of romance. Not today. Today I would rather have none. Why do you allow us to hurt each other this way? Why did you let it happen to me? Yet, through the pain I feel, I also long for the feeling that brought it to me. I long for romance and companionship. I long for a soulmate. God, in your mercy, hear my prayer and give me wisdom someday to select the right person to share life with and the patience to wait until I find them. *Amen.*

Being Without a Boyfriend/Girlfriend:

I know that I am not supposed to base my value on whether or not I am in a romantic relationship with someone else. I know that I'm not supposed to think of myself as lacking when I am not "with" someone. But sometimes it's difficult to be that secure in myself. God, I need to find my identity in you and in who you have created me to be. Will you help me? Please? Help me not feel incomplete. Help me not feel lonely. Help me to remember that not being in a romantic relationship can be a blessing and is far from a curse. Use my time without a boyfriend/girlfriend to bring me closer to you. Use my time without a boyfriend/girlfriend to reach out to those who are hurting. Use my time without a boyfriend/girlfriend to bring more justice, peace, and mercy to my hurting world. *Amen.*

For a Spouse (Someday):

I really feel that you want me to be married. Someday. I know I have a way to go, so—before I get to that moment—will you help me to prepare myself to be a good spouse? Right here where I am right now, as I am establishing who I am as a person in a romantic relationship, give me the courage to avoid the habits of life and relationship that end up making marriage difficult. Protect me from my own wandering heart that wants to latch onto the first promising mate and wants to give me a reason to compromise my morals on something that isn't going to happen for a while. And for whoever it is that I will marry, do the same for them. Prepare them, give them courage, and protect them. May we find each other in a moment of health and happiness and grow into a deep abiding love rooted in our relationship with you. *Amen.*

FOR AN UNPLANNED PREGNANCY

I'm Pregnant:

I'm pregnant. And, I'm not quite sure exactly how to feel right now. Depending on who I tell, I get different advice and a different perspective. All I know right now is that there is a tiny beginning inside me and that kind of blows my mind. Though I don't know what I need to do right now, I know that I need you. I also know that I cannot go through this alone. Will you bring me loving, supportive people to lean on? Will you give me older women who love me and who have been through this to ask questions about the decisions I must make? Will you give me grace to let go of any weird or inappropriate things said to me? Help me enforce good, healthy boundaries and make the choices that protect my heart and my body. And, as I walk this path, may it be one that leads me closer to you. *Amen.*

My Girlfriend Is Pregnant:

She's pregnant. Every time I think about it my mind fills with so many thoughts I don't even know where to start; I don't really know what to do or say. I know I have all kinds of responsibility, yet my body is not the one that's going to change. People will not know just by looking at me, because I'm not the one whose body will change. And it's even possible that most people will have no idea that my shoulders are filling up with weights I have no idea how to bear. God, can you be a guide for me through the maze of emotions and responsibility? Give me the ability to say the right thing when I need to talk and be quiet when that's what I need to do. Give me the right people to lean on when I'm about to fall over. Give me wisdom to know how to support this young woman in what will clearly be more confusing and difficult for her than it will be for me. *Amen.*

FOR WORKING

I Need a Job:

Look, it's not that I don't want to work, but right now I can't because I don't have a job. I have filled out applications, emailed my parents' friends and nothing has happened. On some level it feels petty to be praying about my job when there are people starving, but here I am. I need your help. Help me to remember my connections and have the courage to contact them. Help me notice the job opportunities in my day-to-day life, help me write well and remember to proofread before I submit applications, and give me favor with the people conducting the interviews so that I get the job that will work for my life right now. *Amen.*

First Day of Work:
Thank you, God, for a job! I know there are always people wanting
to work who are unable to for whatever reason, and so I thank you
that I've received the gift of this job. As I get ready to begin, will you
help me get off to a good start? Please help me be a good employee in
my boss's eyes. May my boss see me as a hard worker who is willing
to learn and who will support his/her coworkers. May my boss be
impressed with my ability and my personality. Also, I pray that you
will give me the same sort of rapport with my new coworkers. Will
you help them to feel they can trust me and not be threatened by me?
At the same time, give me wisdom to see past the masks that some
people will wear for me today. Help me see where the dangers lie and
who is worthy of my trust. At the end of this day whether it is perfect
or less than perfect, I will praise you for giving me the gift of a first
day at work. Thank you, God. *Amen.*

FOR LOSS

Death of Family Member:
I can't believe they aren't here anymore. I have all these memories
that feel so much more real than the fact that they are gone. And to
be completely honest I'm pretty angry, and you aren't in the clear
here, God. You could have stopped it, right? But you didn't. And
that's not cool, because I am hurting. There are moments when I'd do
anything to bring them back even for one more day, but I know that's
not possible. So, I'm left with sadness. It comes in waves between
funny memories that make me miss them even more and the sadness
returns. Help me be okay with these emotions. And help me be okay
when there are less of them. But more than that, could you help me to
honor them by being more like all their best qualities? And bring me
peace. *Amen.*

Losing a Pet:
You created animals, and you put a special place in our hearts for
them when you asked us to care for them. I know that because my
heart is hurting now. This pet that you gave me was more than a toy.
My pet was more than a diversion. My pet was how I was caring

for the world, and it was mysteriously also caring for me. God, in my sadness remind me of all the good times and funny moments. Help me heal from this sadness and surround me with people who understand and can put an arm around me when I need it. Because I need it. I miss my pet. *Amen.*

Parents Getting a Divorce:

That's it, God. We have to talk. I'm pretty angry right now. At you. For real. I mean, you created the universe. I hear people tell stories of you performing miracles like healing cancer, but you couldn't fix my parent's marriage. Really? Why not, God? Why not? I know that they aren't happy. I know all the reasons that they said. I know it because I have lived with it, but that doesn't matter. Because you had the power to change it and you didn't. I'm mad and hurt and broken and I feel like the gravity has changed in my world, and I'm stumbling around trying to figure out how to walk again. You know what I want. You know I want this to not happen. All of it. I want all the causes and this crummy outcome to disappear. But If you won't magically change it, will you at least comfort me? Because I'm falling apart. And my parents are so weird right now that I don't even know how to talk to them about all this. Please help me. Please send friends and ministers and teachers and whoever you can to help me. Give me peace in the middle of this tornado that is tearing things apart. Because I need it. I need you. *Amen.*

When a Friend Moves Away:

Seriously? They're moving. My friend is moving? I know it's not something I can control, and it's not really something unusual, but it makes me so irritated. Why do we get close to people only to have them leave? Why is that what happens? I am going to miss them so much. And I know we can stay in touch, but it's not the same. They will move on and so will I, but that makes me sad. So, can you help me replace my irritation and sadness with thankfulness for what we had and what we shared? And, if it's in your will, could you move the planets around, or whatever you have to do, to make us come together again sometime in the future? *Amen.*

I'm Moving Away:

It's my turn now. I've had people move. I've had friends leave, and now, I'm the one. I'm the one that leaving, and it's going to be hard. I'm going to miss all of my favorite places. I'm going to miss the secret spots I've found. I'm going to miss the familiar sounds and smells. But most of all, I'm going to miss the people. I'm going to miss the friends, the teachers, the bosses, the coworkers, and the random shop clerk I have come to know. It's a lot of change. It's a lot of "different," Lord. And that means it hurts right now, a lot. Please God, help me to grieve the loss and celebrate the old, but don't let that keep me from making new friends and enjoying the new place I'm headed. Let me honor the old by enjoying the new. *Amen.*

FOR EVEN MORE...

Being Bullied:

On some level, I'm embarrassed to even pray about this. I'm being bullied, and it hurts, and I want it to stop. For whatever reason it keeps happening. People keep feeling they have the right to wound me and shame me and make me the butt of their jokes. I feel powerless to stop it. After it's over I can think of a thousand things that I could have done or said, but when it's happening nothing I do or say seems to make it stop. I need your protection. I can't take this anymore, and I need my God to rescue me. I'd also kind of like it if you'd make a whale swallow them or even turn them into a pillar of salt maybe. You did that before, right? So, you know, if you still do that kind of thing, I'm okay with it. But for real I need this to stop, and I don't see how to make that happen. Will you do that, God? Will you bring the right person or idea or whatever it will take to make this stop? Will you make these wounds heal? Can you show me how to regain my confidence? And make it stop. Please. *Amen.*

Stress:

Why do I get this way? Why, O God, do I allow myself to fall into this pit and get covered over in stress? But that's where I am. I'm stressed out right now, and I need help. I have tried the things I try, but I still haven't found a way out from under the weight of this stress. Since stress ultimately comes from not feeling in control, will you show my something I can control? Will you show me a decision I can make, and then another? Can you help me find the rungs of the ladder to climb out of this pit of stress so that I can have a clear enough mind to feel like I can follow you? *Amen.*

Difficulty Focusing:

I'm all over the place right now. In fact, I'm not 100% sure I'm going to make it to the end of this prayer. Though being distracted doesn't always bother me, right now it's driving me crazy. So, I need help focusing. I need help to stop the constant scrolling in my mind. Center me, Lord. Help me to let go of all the distractions and be fully present right here, right now. *Amen.*

Before a Performance:

It's time, God. All the practice, all the rehearsals, all the time I have put in comes down to this. God, I pray that I would do my absolute best. For that to happen, I need a little help calming myself. The Bible calls the Holy Spirit the "Comforter" sometimes, and that's what I need. Will you fill me with your Spirit so that I might experience a level of peace and comfort? So that my nerves don't make this performance difficult? I pray that you would make all the effort I have put into everything that has led to this point pay off. I pray that I would do well and that you would be glorified by the way I carry myself before, during, and after. *Amen.*

End of a Retreat/Camp:

Wow. I have been overwhelmed by your presence. I have felt such a deep connection with the other people here. I have been filled with your Spirit and convicted of my sin. Thank you, Lord, for the gift of retreats. But now, it's time to head home. I have to leave this place where life and faith seem to fit together so simply and return to the messiness of my everyday life. God, help me to not turn this retreat and the feelings I've had here into an idol. Help me to not mix up emotions or a certain experience with your presence, which is always with me despite emotions and experiences. Remind me that the real Christian life is lived in between the mountain tops. Help me see this retreat as a special gift from you. Thank you for that gift. Thanks for this retreat. Now I ask that you give me the ability to live my life differently as a result of what you've said to me here and what I experienced. *Amen.*

My Birthday:

As I complete another year on my journey, give me a moment to think back on all that's happened. Give me perspective and insight to evaluate how I did this past year in growing spiritually. I know I'm another year older, but have I grown another year older in my spiritual life? God, send your Spirit to help me remember this past year's ups and downs right now. Over the next year, will you remind me over and over again of your presence? Will you wake me with thoughts of you and how I can serve you? Will you use me to make a difference in my world this year, to move it closer to heaven and away from hell? I commit to listening to you more. Will you help me learn how to recognize your voice amid the noise in my life so that I might get to my next birthday even closer to you? *Amen.*

Regarding Nature:

I stand in awe of your creation. From the overwhelming visual symphony played out in each sunset to the brilliant colors caught up in the songs of the birds in the morning, I am stunned by your work. I am mesmerized seeing seeds sprout and grow, becoming infinitely intricate paintings. And there are billions of them. All around. Under my feet, between the cracks in my driveway, and hanging from the branches of other trees that have been growing for ages. In this work of art, you've given me all I need to live—even coffee. You speak to me, over and over, through nature—especially when I remember to look up from my phone. No Instagram filter comes close to what I see in a single cloud. I look up at the clear night sky and see the billions of places that you have created that I will never know, yet you, who created all of this, care about me. You love me, and most shocking of all, you are listening to me right now as I pray. Thank you. Thank you for provision, for beauty, for things that make me humble. Thank you for nature. *Amen.*

I Got a New Thing:

Thank you, God, for _____. I know that everything I have ultimately comes from you, because you are the Creator of all things. I ask you to help this magnify the good things in my life and myself and not magnify the bad. I ask that you would guard my heart against consumerism. As I enjoy this thing, help me not to use it to just desire more and more stuff. Give me the courage to say no to greed and gluttony and be content with what I have so that my life can focus on you instead of material things. *Amen.*

LESS WORDS,
MORE PRAYER

LESS WORDS, MORE PRAYER
(ANCIENT PRAYER PRACTICES)

Up to this point I have given you thousands of words to help you express your heart to God and guide you in a conversation with your Creator. However, words aren't always the answer when it comes to prayer. In fact, there are several faith traditions within Christianity that would say your logical mind can get in the way of experiencing the presence of God at the deepest levels.

For centuries people have sought out ways to let go of all that distracts so that they could experience the presence of God with far fewer words than you have found here, but I've decided to let go of offering you the history of these methods in favor of simply instructing you in their practice. If you connect with any of these mystical prayer practices, they all have rich Christian faith stories behind them that will help you grow to enjoy them even more if you choose to explore further. A simple Google search of "Christian Centering Prayer" or the other prayers listed here will yield more than enough, but if you'd like to have a good book on the subject, I recommend *The Sacred Way: Spiritual Practices for Everyday Life* (Emergent YS/Zondervan, 2005).

Centering Prayer

At the root of Centering Prayer is the conviction that our cluttered minds are the ultimate distraction from entering a state of divine union with God. This practice seeks to teach people learn to let go of all that is cluttering their minds until all that is left is the individual resting in the presence of God.

The Trappist monk and Christian mystic Thomas Keating uses the metaphor of a river. (*The Contemplative Journey: Contemplation and Transformation from Christianity's Mystical Tradition*, Sounds True, Inc., 2005.) If you imagine your mind being like a river with each thought being a boat on the river, you'll quickly recognize that your river is rather full at any given moment. For most of us, our river is so full of random thoughts, it can't move along. We get stuck in patterns of over-focusing on unimportant thoughts and don't spend enough time on the important ones. The goal of Centering Prayer is to clear the river of the backlog of boats until only one boat remains: God.

We begin to do that by selecting a sacred word. It should be one or two syllables and mean God for you. It may be *God* or *Lord* or another word that symbolizes God. You chose the word. Then you begin to clear the river of your mind by sitting still and trying to relax. Still and relaxed, you center yourself on the word. Whenever a thought invades your mind, you simply answer the thought with your word and let it pass. You continue doing that until the only thing that is left in your mind is the one word. Having achieved that state of clarity, you try to then let go of the one word and rest in the presence of God.

I will say that this is not easy. It can take a long time to ever be able to get to this final state especially in a world that has become completely comfortable with constant distraction. Don't worry if you can't quite get there the first time or two. And give yourself time to practice.

Centering Prayer is not a one-minute exercise. The first time, make your goal at least ten, if not fifteen, minutes. Try to increase the length each time until you become more comfortable with the process.

I've found that this prayer practice not only helps me center myself on God, but it also helps develop my ability to quiet my mind. Much like doing repetitive exercises at a gym will help you develop physically, this will help build the mental muscle that gives you the ability to focus and be fully present. Now that you have the basics, use these instructions to help guide you through the practice. Once you've done it a couple times you will most likely not need these instructions, as it is relatively simple.

1. **Sit.** Sit in a relaxed posture with your eyes closed enough to not be distracted by what you see, but not closed so far that you are tempted to fall asleep.

2. **Breathe.** Pay attention to your breathing. Take several slow, deep breaths trying to exhale slowly.

3. **Choose.** Choose the word that helps you focus on God.

4. **Focus.** Take up the word as the focus of your thoughts. As

other thoughts demand your attention, simply answer them with the word and let them pass.

5. **Rest.** Once you have let go of all the invasive thoughts, let go even of the word and rest in the presence of God.

6. **Return.** Begin paying attention to your surroundings again and finish your prayer time by saying the Lord's Prayer.

The Jesus Prayer

We move from the most difficult to the most simple. Where Centering Prayer focuses on quieting your mind so that you can be centered on God, the Jesus Prayer focuses on occupying your mind with a simple prayer so that you can fully experience the presence of God.

This is done by saying the prayer "Lord Jesus Christ, Son of God, have mercy on me a sinner" over and over again. The prayer is spoken in the rhythm of your breathing. As you breathe in you say, "Lord Jesus Christ, Son of God," and as you breathe out you say, "have mercy on me a sinner." You will do this over and over for a specific number of repetitions.

Though you can keep count on your fingers or in your head, it can be helpful to use a piece of rope or string with knots in it to help you count. You can make one easily by taking the rope, tying nine knots in a row and then tying the two ends together with a square knot. As you pray, you move your fingers to hold the next knot and then the next after each time your complete a repetition of the prayer. Then once you reach the larger square knot at the end, you know you have said the prayer ten times.

I encourage people to take the time to say the prayer 200 times (about 15 minutes) on their first try and then increase as much as you can each time after that. After giving this powerful tool to a sixth-grade boy several years ago, I was pumped when he showed up at my office a week later saying that he had made a larger rope (with 100 knots) because he had reached 1500 repetitions! He had not only experienced the prayer, but experienced the moment when his mind was on auto pilot and he became aware of his spirit communing with God.

Like Centering Prayer, this practice also has unintended positive side effects. A good friend of mine named Jean Tippit decided to try to do a thousand or more every day. To do that, she had to be really intentional about scheduling time to do it. What she didn't realize was how deeply that prayer was being planted within her.

A couple weeks later, Jean was completely stressed out and had someone walk up to her at church to complain about something. On any other day it would have been fine. She would have been kind and attentive and would have worked together with the person on a solution. But not that day. She'd had almost no sleep in a week because of a host of reasons, and she snapped. She opened her mouth to yell at the person, but instead of her angry words coming out, she yelled, "Lord Jesus Christ, Son of God, have mercy on me a sinner." She was shocked to say the least. Her outburst made her realize that she was going to overreact, and she regrouped to address the person much more calmly. Beyond that one situation, she was amazed that using this prayer had helped form her heart so deeply that her anger came out as a prayer.

I don't think you'll start yelling this prayer at your enemies any time soon, but this practice is great because it can flow so easily into the rest of your life. You can pray it on the road on the way to your first day at work, you can say it as you are walking to the classroom at school, you can say it at night as you fall asleep.

Now, let me walk you through it, but like the last, you'll get the idea eventually and won't need the book.

1. **Sit.** Sit in a relaxed posture with your eyes closed enough to not be distracted by what you see, but not closed so far that you are tempted to fall asleep.

2. **Breathe.** Pay attention to your breathing. Take several slow, deep breaths trying to exhale slowly.

3. **Inhale.** Then take up the prayer saying, "Lord Jesus Christ, Son of God..."

4. **Exhale.** Then as you breathe out say, "...have mercy on me a sinner."

Lectio Divina
Lectio Divina is built on the confidence that whenever you read the

Bible, God is speaking to you. However, Lectio Divina approaches hearing God's voice in a unique way. Rather than digging deep into the meaning of a specific passage or trying to understand the original cultural context of a selection, Lectio Divina focuses on the words themselves and uses them as a focus point to help center yourself on God's voice.

Lectio Divina treats the Bible the same way you would a small portion of the most tasteful dessert you've ever had. Instead of taking it all in one bite, you take it bit by bit and savor each taste. As you practice Lectio Divina, instead of taking it all in one bite, you will proceed slowly savoring each word.

In Lectio Divina, there are four major movements. It begins with reading the text in a way you have likely never read it before. After selecting a passage in the Bible, you will begin to read it as slowly as possible so that you can savor every word. After you have read the entire passage as slowly as possible, you begin again reading the passage slowly, word by word. You repeat this process over and over enjoying each new idea, each new perspective as it comes to your mind in this slow, repetitive reading.

As you read it slowly, there will be some word or phrase that seems to be particularly notable. For some people, they experience not being able to move past a word and feel like they sort of get stuck in a place each time they read. Others talk about a word seeming to shimmer. As you read there will be a word that particularly catches your attention. This word is "shimmering" because God wants to use it to speak. You continue then with your shimmering word to the next movement.

The second movement focuses on experiencing the word. This one can be especially difficult for those of us who have been taught how to quickly begin thinking about the implications of words and ideas. It is difficult because thinking about the implications of this word must be held off until the third movement. In the second, we simply repeat the word over and over and experience what that word does inside our hearts and minds. *What emotions does it bring up? What thoughts are connected to it? What memories surround it?* Repeat the word and allow the Holy Spirit to bring relevant connected thoughts and emotions to the front of your mind and heart.

The third movement is time spent in prayer with God. Here it is important to both speak and listen. You might ask God why this word shimmered. You might ask why you feel the way you do when you meditate on the word or what action God is asking you to take as a result. The goal is to ask questions and wait for answers to come to your mind. This is the analyzing moment when you try to discover what it is that God is saying to you.

Finally, you use the word you've chosen as your sacred word for Centering Prayer and use it to enter into a time of contemplative prayer. The goal here is to let go of all of the active prayer and rest in God. (See **Centering Prayer** instructions on page 195.)

Practicing Lectio Divina should take while. It is best to try and devote even amounts of time to each movement so that you don't rush past one for another. Most people need help with the time portion, so try setting a timer on your phone or something like that your first several attempts. This may be the mystical practice that, in my experience, seems to get the most immediate positive response from people. It seems to make the Bible come alive in completely new ways and is active enough to not seem too foreign to the western mind. For your first try, I think you can have an amazing first experience by devoting five minutes to each movement. Let's get started!

1. **Sit.** Sit in a relaxed posture with your eyes closed enough to not be distracted by what you see, but not closed so far that you are unable to read.

2. **Read.** Open the Bible and read your passage slowly and repeatedly savoring each word. While you read, look for a word or phrase that attracts your attention and "shimmers."

3. **Consider.** Now begin to consider your word or phrase. Ask: *What emotions does it bring up? What other memories are associated with it?* Be careful not to begin analyzing the implication of all these things, but merely experience them as you repeat your word or phrase.

4. **Ask.** Now it's time to have a conversation with God. Ask: *Why this word? What is God trying to tell me?*

5. **Pray/Rest.** Finish by taking the word up as your sacred word and entering into a time of contemplative prayer. Clear

your mind and rest in the presence of God.

Ignatian Examen

Examining our hearts in the presence of God is a central part of the spiritual life. Saint Ignatius created a method for doing that and published it in 1548. It is an expression of the deep need of all believers expressed in Psalm 139:23, "Search me, O God, and know my heart; test me and know my anxious thoughts." Saint Ignatius first imagined this method as the basis for a retreat, but it has since turned into a daily practice where we allow the Holy Spirit to guide us through a reflection of our day, celebrating with God and asking for forgiveness.

As with many of these practices, the Ignatian Examen happens in multiple movements (five, to be precise).

The Examen begins with thanking God for all the good things in your life and in the previous day while also asking the Holy Spirit to search you as you reflect on your day.

The second movement focuses on the ability to recognize sin. We often play a game with ourselves where we find great excuses for our sin or ignore our faults altogether. If you have ever had someone call you out on something you did wrong, you'll notice that most often your first response—if you're like the rest of us—is to defend yourself and justify your actions rather than naming the sins and asking for forgiveness. What is even more tragic than our denial to other people is that we do the same thing within ourselves. We go through a lot of life justifying our sins to ourselves rather than owning them and beginning to live differently. The second movement stands in direct opposition to that denial. In this movement, you ask God to help you not ignore or pass over your sins but to give you the grace to know and rid your heart of them.

The third movement is the real focus of the Examen and occupies the lion's share of the time. In this movement, we ask the Spirit to guide us throughout our day, hour by hour, and point out the sin in our lives. We begin at the moment we woke up and continue replaying our day bit by bit until we reach the end. When we find a moment where we sinned, we pause to enter into that moment in deeper reflection. We try to experience what was happening. *What emotions were present in the moment? What emotions are you feeling now as you remember it? How might God be speaking to you through the emotions?*

The fourth movement is to ask for forgiveness. It is as simple as it sounds. Armed with all the places where you walked away from what God calls you to do and who God calls you to be, you ask God to forgive you for your sin.

The final movement looks forward. We ask God to show us the way to walk from where we are into the future. We consider each way we sinned and ask God to show us how we can live differently tomorrow. Most people finish this prayer time by praying the Lord's Prayer.

If there is one thing that is most often missing from my life, it is serious reflection. I spend a minute or two here or there, but when I read about the Examen, my heart wakes up because I long for this level of reflection. I need it. Let's walk through it together:

1. **Express gratefulness.** Thank God for all the good things, and then ask the Holy Spirit to guide you as you begin to reflect on the day.

2. **Be open-hearted.** Ask God to give you the ability to see your sins plainly and not ignore or justify them.

3. **Review your day.** Begin playing your day back and pay attention to each moment where you sinned. Enter into these moments. Ask: *What was I feeling in that moment? What am I feeling now?*

4. **Seek forgiveness.** Ask for forgiveness for each sin.

5. **Press on.** Begin to figure out how you can, with God's help, live differently tomorrow. Ask: *How can I avoid sinning in the same way as today?*

USING THIS BOOK
IN A GROUP SETTING

USING THIS BOOK IN A GROUP SETTING
(FOR LEADERS)

"Who wants to open us up in prayer?" Silence. Crickets. Discomfort. "Not everyone at once..." More silence. Then, Addison, who is always the one who prays, steps up to the plate again sounding disappointed: "I'll do it I guess."

The prayer time in a group setting can turn into one of the most uncomfortable moments as people avoid eye contact with the leader, so that they don't get "voluntold" to do it. But it's the ideas underneath that tension that are even more troubling. One of the main reasons that people don't want to volunteer to pray in your group is that they don't know what to say and/or are afraid they might say something wrong or stupid.

A lot of that is caused by a fear of spontaneous public speaking. This book can help. First, armed with all the prayers for specific moments, the participants in the group can be asked to read a prayer instead of coming up with something off the top of their heads that is both coherent and spiritual. Moreover, as we read prayers that have been written by other people, we learn how to express the depths of our own hearts to God. I like to think of this book as helping equip people with a sort of prayer vocabulary, so that when they sit down to pray throughout their day, they feel confident they have a place to start.

After using this book in various group settings from teens to college students to older adults, I can tell you that, when done right, it is very powerful. On the other hand, if you don't do a couple of simple things, the results are a mixed bag. That's what this chapter is all about: giving you the nuts and bolts to put this into practice in a group setting so that the prayer service doesn't fall flat.

THE ELEMENTS OF EACH SERVICE
In each prayer service you'll find the following:

- **Call to Prayer:** There is something deep within us that calls us to prayer. The Call to Prayer reminds us that we pray not because we want something but because God is worthy of prayer and there is something deep within us that longs to reach out and connect. Generally, these calls reflect something about God that is worthy of praise.

- **Invitation:** From the earliest days, when people began praying to God, they asked for God to be present. Sometimes in Scripture we see people asking God to remember his covenant and sometimes we see his people just crying out, asking God to listen. The Invitation asks for God to be present, to listen, and to respond.

- **Confession**: When we enter God's presence we immediately come face to face with our own brokenness. That's why confession is an important part of these services. Several have a time for you to take a moment to think through your sins and confess them specifically, while others offer a more general confession.

- **Refrain:** The Refrain gives focus and grounds the rest of the prayer for participants. As you read, think of how the Refrain connects to the Reading and the Psalm and the rest of the elements.

- **Reading:** Prayer is a two-way street. We talk to God, but God also talks to us. When God speaks, it can come to us like a thought in our heads, but it can also be in the words of another person or in something we read (especially the Bible). Think of the Reading as one of the ways that God could be speaking to your group.

- **Psalm:** Art helps us express things that are bigger than we are. It helps us express our love, our fears, and our biggest hopes. This section takes poetry composed by brilliant writers throughout history to help us reach out and express our hearts to God.

- **The Lord's Prayer:** I have chosen to print the version here that is in an older form of English (adapted from *The Book of Common Prayer*). I have done that because the older sounding words help remind us we are saying a prayer that is very old; in fact, it is the oldest Christian prayer we have.

- **Today's Prayer:** Each day has a prayer that's tied to that specific moment in the week and helps express a hope and challenge for what that moment in a week brings.

- **Concluding Prayer:** Each service also concludes with a prayer that tries to express something specific for that time of the day on that day of the week. You'll find that Evening Prayers often talk about going to sleep while Dawn Prayers talk about the beginning of a new day.

USING "PRAYERS THROUGHOUT THE DAY" IN A GROUP SETTING

Adapting these prayer experiences to a group setting is pretty straightforward, but these tips should help you leverage your group meeting to bring these prayer services to life.

Go slow. Remember this is about listening and talking!

Before you begin the prayer portion of your gathering, take a moment to remind your group that prayer is a conversation, and that means we need to build times of listening into our prayers. You need to go slow and take significant pauses throughout each service to open up space for your group to listen to God and center themselves. If you aren't careful, you will find yourself treating these services like tasks you need to complete rather than conversations. Don't rush. Don't blow through them. Take your time. It's better to not finish than to reach the end without ever stopping to listen.

Encourage the group to pause between each section for as long as is comfortable to them. That rhythm of silence will push against the feeling that we have to fill all the empty space with words. Though the regular silence can feel a little uncomfortable at times, don't change it. That uncomfortableness with silence and space between things is unhealthy (particularly when it comes to prayer), and you need to do your best to equip your participants to fight it. If it seemed especially uncomfortable, recognize that at the end of the prayer service. Take a moment to process the uneasiness that was felt, being careful to lift up the value of silence and listening in a healthy prayer life.

Have many voices read aloud.

This is where the group setting can take these prayers to a new level. I like to use a unique person for every section (with the same person reading the refrain everywhere it appears), with me leading the Lord's Prayer and the Concluding Prayer. Since the Refrain is repeated a handful of times throughout the service, asking a single person to read it over and over again can reflect that sense of echo more audibly. This can bring so much life and meaning as each person reads with their own take on the prayer, bringing their own perspective and emotion to it.

Don't feel bound to the order and words.

Feel free to make this your own and use these prayer services as a starting point for your own services. Add your own prayers or have a time for groups to make their own requests to God regarding a specific situation. You might also choose a particularly appropriate prayer from the **Right Words for the Right Time** section (page 177) and add it into the service.

How about making a weekend out of it?

One of my favorite retreats was what we called the Silence and Solitude Retreat. It was exactly that. It was a weekend filled with silence and solitude and prayer. For that weekend, we took 36 hours and made sure to spend well over half of them in intentional prayer. We woke up at midnight for midnight prayer; walked outside at dawn and did the Dawn Prayer time together as we watched the sun rise. We did every one of the hours prescribed here and then did some of the mystical prayer practices in the **Less Words, More Prayer** section (page 193) in between the appointed prayer service times. Here's a rough schedule that you could use to make a weekend out of this:

Silence and Solitude Retreat Schedule

11:00	AM	Arrive and Unload
11:30	AM	Lunch
12:00	PM	Noonday Prayer
12:30	PM	Play
1:30	PM	Centering Prayer
2:30	PM	Afternoon Prayer
3:30	PM	Lectio Divina
4:30	PM	Play
6:00	PM	Dinner
7:00	PM	Play

9:00	PM	Personal Study/Ignatian Examen
10:00	PM	End of Day Prayer
12:00	AM	Midnight Prayer
3:00	AM	Night Watch Service
5:57	AM	Dawn Prayer
6:15	AM	The Jesus Prayer
8:00	AM	Morning Prayer
9:00	AM	Breakfast
10:00	AM	Play
11:30	AM	Lunch
12:00	PM	Noonday Prayer
1:00	PM	Go Home

There it is. All you need for a prayer retreat. I hope this book does more than give you a great retreat. My hope is that as you introduce others to the book, you are introducing them to a life of prayer in general. I pray that as they become comfortable with the book, they spend more and more of each day with God, filling the hours with prayer.

MY PRAYERS

MY PRAYERS

MY PRAYERS

MY PRAYERS

MY PRAYERS

MY PRAYERS

MY PRAYERS

MY PRAYERS

MY PRAYERS

Made in United States
Orlando, FL
29 March 2022

16271506R00122